The Real Log Cabin

The Real Log Cabin

Original Text by Chilson D. Aldrich
Expanded with Commentary by Harry Drabik

NODIN PRESS

Library of Congress Catalog Card No. 90-92230
ISBN 0-931714-51-6

Nodin Press, a division of Micawber's, Inc.
525 North Third Street
Minneapolis, MN 55401

Printed in the U.S.A. at
Printing Enterprises, Minneapolis, MN

Snail cabin drawings on page 156 reprinted courtesy
the Ministry of Culture and Communications,
Province of Ontario.
Additional drawings by
Alexander Rymarowicz, Krakow, Poland

This edition is dedicated with love and deep respect to
Tymie Randall
without whose support, faith, and trust this project
would never have seen completion.

THE RED GODS' CALL

"I'm tired of the rustle and hustle,
I'm sick of the racket and din,
I want to cut loose from the bustle,
Go out where the rivers begin.
I long to get up in the open,
'Mongst the cedar and tall tamarack;
I want to make camp on a lake shore;
In an old tumble-down lumber shack.
I'm tired of the pomp and grandeur,
I'm sick of the falseness and bluff;
I want to get up where the country
Is virgin and wooded and rough.
I long to awake in the morning,
And pull on an old flannel shirt,
And corduroy pants that are mended
And moccasins covered with dirt.
I care not a cuss where the place is,
Nor how far away it may be,
So long as it's up in the open
Where I can unleash and be free.
Where the odor of cedar and hemlock
Will greet me whene'er I awake,
And the moon casts its shadows at nightfall
Of the pine on the wind-rippled lake.
Just give me my pipe and tobacco,
Some coffee and bacon, and then
Turn me foot-loose away in the forest,
Far off from the pathways of men."

INTRODUCTION

We have decided to reissue *The Real Log Cabin* in a version close to its original form, even where it was tempting to eliminate or streamline parts of the text, in order to preserve the flavor of its time. Whether Chilson Darragh Aldrich has much to say for our day will be settled by his new readers, but after it was first published by Macmillan in 1928, *The Real Log Cabin* became popular enough to stay in print for more than two decades. Earlier generations began to admire and emulate rural life as America became more urban, and Aldrich addressed that aspect of the American imagination.

Reprinting an old book presents special problems. Some consider this book "too male dominated." Others characterize the type of log work that Aldrich describes as "too simple." I agree, but I have mostly retained the warts and blemishes of this historic book. *The Real Log Cabin*, like most things, is far from perfect. This new edition of *The Real Log Cabin* includes most of Aldrich's text, plus my commentary in italic, to update every chapter. Because many of the old photos were inadequate, we've added drawings. With this expanded edition, I hope readers will find inspiration and a connection with the past, with an improved understanding of what summer homes once meant and how they have been transformed over the years.

Harry F. Drabik

October, 1993

FOREWORD

It is being increasingly borne in upon the members of the present generation that they have lost much by not being pioneers. Much in the stuff that goes to make character. Much of the downright exhilarating fun.

With increasing frequency, therefore, one finds that the genuine American is going back to the good old ancestral custom—bootlegging his pioneer kick as it were—and building himself a log cabin away from the honks of man. This "cabin" varies all the way from a modest little one room (without kitchenette and bath) to a log house as many-chambered, as bespattered with baths, as piped and wired and garaged as a townhouse of the most fastidious. Until it becomes the problem how to camouflage these concessions to the softer life. How, in spite of them, to present the appearance of the rugged pioneer home. This requires not only the technique of the architect with his knowledge of residence needs, nor alone the skill of the woodsman with his cunning craft in selecting, cutting and fitting logs—but somehow a blending of the two. Ruggedness must mean lines of strength, not mere uncouthness, and beauty of structure must harmonize with the sturdy material in which it is wrought.

Except for the knowledge of a few of our newly arrived citizens-to-be, fresh from the forests of the old country, log work is almost a lost art. And then there are the architectural problems. For a novice to secure even passable results in meeting the manifold problems that arise when one starts to work in logs requires a lot of experimenting and a good many baffling failures. For those who have not time to experiment and possibly fail, this book is written.

It is not to be denied that the "I's," "We's," "My's," and "Our's" are scattered with a lavish hand throughout the chapters. But be keen enough and kind enough, You Who Read, to realize that these are not egotistical signs. Quite the contrary. Herein are revealed ways of planning and building log cabins—ways learned by the perspiration of one's forehead. There may be other ways. Therefore to make the grandiose statement, "This must be done thus and thus," would smack of egotism indeed. It would assume that the last word is writ herein. It isn't. We—meaning this time the human race—are only beginning to comprehend the beauty that can be wrought of logs. The majority of people assume, without overtaxing their gray matter by reasoning, that any brawny woodsman let loose with an ax where there are plenty of trees can build a log cabin.

Although I had not precisely that notion when I decided to build a cabin for myself, I did hold to the opinion that an architect with twenty years' experience of fine residence work back of him ought to know enough to put up a one-room log cabin. So—I began to build our first permanent home in the woods.

Well—to paraphrase Kipling, "I learned about cabins from her." In fact, the paraphrase might be pushed into further stanzas with equal precision, for in ten years of study and work devoted entirely to homes which can be wrought of logs, each building has taught me something about cabins which I did not know before.

If these experiences and suggestions of mine solve a few of your problems for you, and thereby help you to build nearer your heart's desire, this book has served its sole purpose.

CHILSON D. ALDRICH.

April, 1928

CONTENTS

BOOK ONE
PREPARATION

BOOK TWO
CONSTRUCTION

THE WISTFUL VERSE THAT BEGAN IT

I wish we might go gypsying, dear lad, the while we care—
The while we've heart for hazarding,
The while we've will to sing,
The while we've wit to hear the call
And youth and mirth to spare,
Before a day may find us too sad for gypsying,
Before a day may find us too dull to dream and dare—
I wish we might go gypsying, dear lad, the while we care!

—THEODOSIA GARRISON.

BOOK ONE

PREPARATION

THE REAL LOG CABIN

CHAPTER ONE

LET US GO A-GYPSYING

In my extremely brief and unsatisfactory study of Latin—because the high school course required it—there was only one person who seemed to me to have a few regular human feelings. Why in thunder Julius Caesar should want to fight all the time—and why in double thunder he should want to write about his wars, and why in triple thunder anybody should want to read about them, even if written in English, passed my comprehension. My private opinion of Cicero was that he was a conceited old bore who talked entirely too much in public about people he did not like. But the fellow who came on after him. I could understand the gentleman by the name of Quintus Horatius Flaccus even though he considered himself a poet.

Signor Flaccus—or to get right down to chumminess at once, Friend Horace—sounded to me a lot like a Boy Scout. He believed in the out-of-door life. Already—in the early thirties B.C. he was longing for a return of the good old times when a man was not harassed by the shackles of civilization. (Which meant to me that he did not have to wear a tie and could spread a whole piece of bread at once if he liked.)

Translation was easy. Not that I knew Latin, but I knew Friend Horace. I could tell exactly what he was going to say. Not only did I render his feelings in my mother tongue with great gusto, but I interpolated a few sentiments of my own. These a narrow-minded professor repudiated for the inadequate reason that they did not appear in the original. Anyway, I made Quint Flaccus a regular fellow. Yet in my heart he created a poignant yearning. With a vast envy I envied him. Not his literary triumphs—Heavens, no! Though two thousand years have

Although dated and in some ways beside the point, this first chapter sets a tone and introduces Chilson Aldrich, who, once he'd moved to Hovland on the north shore of Lake Superior, preferred to be called Stooge. No doubt Stooge acquired this nickname when he was still a boy struggling with Latin in the old grammar schools. But Stooge was no dummy. He valued practical knowledge and skills such as architecture, which he studied and later practiced successfully in Minneapolis, Minnesota.

His marriage came somewhat late in life, after he was established enough as an architect to design and build a home to his new wife's tastes. Located in Minneapolis on Kenwood Parkway, the house was his wedding present to her, and it was an important symbol of their life together, from her crocus stained-glass windows to his fireplace in the living room, where they stood to be joined in matrimony. Mrs. Aldrich was a successful playwright and a radio broadcaster for WCCO in Minneapolis. She discarded her first name, Clara, and adopted her husband's middle name, becoming Darragh Aldrich.

Aldrich's first chapter is full of the romantic zest that inspired their summers in the north. They spent their first summer tenting on their land and then built their first cabin, called Trailsyde. Both seemed to thrive there. During the decade after the First World War, Stooge designed and built six more cabins along the shore, including his wife's tiny writing studio perched at the edge of a cliff overlooking Lake Superior. She named the cabin the Crow's Nest in honor of her brother in the navy. Over the window beside her portable typewriter was the inscription "WHERE IT IS A DELIGHT TO WRITE." The last time repairs were made on her little cabin, we found an incomplete manuscript of a play in the bottom of a storage box.

While Darragh was writing, Stooge was developing the surrounding property to sell to vacationers who shared his brand of sophisticated rustication. He also contributed to the construction of an eighth cabin, Squantum, which was the brainchild of another Minneapolis architect, Maurice Maine. They called the area Pal's Cove, although it didn't always live up to its name: occasionally the pals disagreed over some facet of lifestyle. For example, the first person to have a road built to a cabin was considered a traitor. Stooge's original intent was that people would leave their cars at the highway and walk to their cabins, an act symbolic of leaving behind the hectic, workaday world. But although the first driveway to a cabin caused quite a stir among the other cabin owners, before long they followed that lead, convenience winning out over philosophy. On the whole, however, these talented and affluent people were dedicated to the Aldrich view of rustic living. At first they happily trundled their groceries along dirt paths through the woods. They didn't consider electricity for their summer retreats until after 1950: they spent their evenings around keronsene lamps. Instead of calling a servant, they had to rely on one another for everyday tasks.

established pretty definitely the fact that he wielded no mean stylus in satire and also that he watched his feet pretty carefully in meter.

It is when I read of that plutocrat Maecenas placing him "above the anxieties of a literary life" and presenting him casually—offhand—just like that—with a Sabine farm because he talked so much about wanting one, that even now I rise to a point of disorder in my envy of him. The good old custom of presenting farms to people who are tired of city life ought never to have been allowed to fall into disrepute. Time came— and very shortly—when I could not have told you a word that Horace wrote, but I never forgot Maecenas and that farm.

Wealthy patrons drifted in and out of the office where I bent above a drawing board. To many of them I frankly confided my dislike of the shackles of civilization, but none of them offered to place me above the anxieties of a draftsman's life. Later I chatted with others along this line when I was superintending their extremely sophisticated residences. Most of them I discovered amazedly had a hankering similar to mine. I received lots of sympathy but no farm.

I tried to content myself with a month off in the summer—envied by the rest who dared take only two weeks—poking the nose of my canoe into remote lakes. Then I scrambled back at the end of the month to work overtime for the other eleven in order to get caught up.

I might still be proceeding along this routine, but that one day something happened to me. I married a woman who loved the out-of-doors just about as much as I did. Moreover—and this was a very important point—she felt that life in the open was worth what it cost.

Our honeymoon was a canoe trip in Northern Minnesota and Canada. I took her to my old haunts to show her the beauties I had discovered.

Of the forest homes that we have had none can ever compare with the first one—an upturned canoe over our heads. This is the only home which offers the widest possible latitude for a proper view of the stars and the tree tops. But there are occasions when it does not afford the necessary protection from the weather or four-footed night prowlers.

So there were times when a tent made to my design seemed a better shelter. This design was thoroughly approved of by the Bow Paddle because it had, as she observed, a nice front porch. We found this stretched-out fourth wall a great convenience, as it could be utilized even for protecting a small fire from rain and we could cook our meals without the water from the trees dripping down our backs. (There are unquestionably a few disadvantages of the life in the open that civilization has overcome to one's greater comfort.) This was our second home, and in making a beginning of describing homes in the out-of-doors we should feel a traitor to the cause if we lost sight of the fact that a tent can be made mighty comfortable and cozy. Nothing can approach the sense of supreme well-being that comes after a hard day's paddling when, flooded with heartening warmth by a cup of tea, and satisfied with innumerable rashers of bacon and breakings of bannock, one drops weariedly upon soft blankets heaped upon balsam boughs for the happy dreamless sleep of a child.

Moreover, nothing with any degree of permanence has the tang of adventure equal to that of pulling up stakes each morning, rolling your home into a convenient size for the canoe in the exciting knowledge that it will be unrolled at sunset and put up amid surroundings you have never seen before. For one knows always upon a canoe voyage that just around the next bend is the loveliest land of all!

Yet—as the honeymoon voyage was succeeded by other canoe trips, we found ourselves filled with delight when we visited certain of the old camp sites that we had loved and lost awhile. We felt as if we owned them, and more and more disliked tearing ourselves away from a spot we had cherished. Instead of the lure of pushing on into the Unknown, we occasionally felt almost as abused as Little Joe who was always told to move on.

We began to quote to each other that overworked bit of Kipling:

> "For to admire an' for to see,
> For to be'old this world so wide—
> It never done no good to me,
> But I can't drop it if I tried!"

We wondered if we ought not to try to stop it while the stopping was good.

We loved discovering new waterfalls. But even more we began to realize that we loved resting beside one we had come to know and care for. However different the assembling of them in various places, rocks were always rocks and trees were trees. It seemed to us that much greater interest was to be found in their changing aspects under light and shade than in their differing locations. What infinite variety was to be discovered in the play of sunlight upon a lake which we well knew! In our

North Shore of Lake Superior

Crow's Nest Cabin

day's journeyings there were shallow vistas for which we cared no more than for shallow people. Why waste time on them? We greeted them gaily, hid our chagrin in finding they had no more for us than we could gather at a passing glance, and went on our way to rest in a grove of brooding white pines or to view a sunset from the top of a hill.

Slowly grew upon us, two very important realizations. It seemed to us that most of the ills of body and soul could be cured by one's dwelling for some part of his years among things that are instinct with primal life. Things in which health and strength and beauty abound. Things that grow instead of being builded. Things that pour out in notes that are untutored the heavenly joyousness of being alive. Things that the Greatest Out-of-Door Man of all the ages said "belonged unto our peace." Life is more contagious than disease. That first.

The other was by way of being an admission. Youth was for roving, for adventuring, for risking one's life to see a new arrangement of familiar matters. Old age is for sitting wrapped up in comfort unwilling to bestir itself though the wonder of the world lay at its door. But the Time Between—the golden blossoming time of the spirit that all long to hold fast—what was its desire?

Long ago a poet had sung it. Omar could not have been a youth when he wrote:

> "A jug of wine, a loaf of bread—and Thou
> Beside me singing in the wilderness—"

Such a wilderness would not have been "paradise enow" for youth of the Occident, at any rate. Youth would be up and doing—not sitting under a tree philosophizing. Philosophy is an aspect of this Time Between. That—let one whisper it—is also the time for true romance. When tawdry imitations have lost their allure. When we long with a mighty desire for Reality. When we realize that the years are racing by. Now if ever we must seek the life that will bring with it the thrill of being all we can be.

There may be those who can achieve this thrill selling real estate or radios all the year round—or in getting one's fellow men out of legal difficulties, or in playing bridge. For these, life in the open is what might be called a closet drama.

There is many a way of having fun. For fun is merely each one's most joyous contact with Life. Mine happens to be letting go of civilization and taking to the woods. When I am gone, it will be inscribed upon my tombstone—"This chap was not rated very high financially, but he had a darn good time."

As for giving suggestions on how to live the wild life and urging my fellow men to undertake it for a part of each year at least, I began it at the early age of seven the first night I slept outside in a tent—and I shall undoubtedly be coming back down the trail of future years to answer questions put to me on the Ouija board about it. If you are the sort that grows panicky at the point where the paving ends, this book is not for you.

To each one who longs to dwell in the wilderness, his home is to be a House of Dreams. And comparatively few there are who see it material-ize. Not that I wish to decry dreams. On the contrary. Anybody who has developed anything as far as a sure enough dream has a mighty good start. It is not in the least a bad idea to locate one's dream house in imag-ination first. Such a home site is inexpensive in upkeep and gives one time to mull over one's innermost—and therefore realest—longings. Any one who has located his dream house carefully, and almost given his mind's eye astigmatism by regarding it closely, is going to be pretty clear about it all when he gets ready to build. He is not going to choose to build on a mountain side and then spend the rest of his natural life cussing himself for not choosing a lake shore.

But along with holding your dream house in statu quo, don't begin the same old whimper of waiting until you have time and money to make it materialize. That time never comes. Honest to goodness now, did you ever know anybody who waited until he got the time and money that ever did anything? I never did.

One morning I found in my shaving glass a bit of magazine verse. The sort of thing that the literary call "fugitive verse." (I had a pretty fair idea of how it "fugited" to my looking glass.)

"I wish we might go gypsying . . . the while we care . . ."

Somehow that pesky line sunk in deep. I realized that we were spending the precious time of later youth in doing things that we didn't want to do in order that we could do the things we wanted to do when we were too old to want to do them.

Anyhow—that bit of verse began the history of our Trailsyde Cabin, the nucleus of the little group along the glorious strip of beach and for-est and tumbled rocky headlands on the North Shore of Lake Superior.

With a limitless view over "Sky-blue Water."

CHAPTER TWO

THE SITE

First catch your site.

Nobody but yourself and the "Thou" who is to sit beside you in the wilderness can divine precisely what you long for. Least of all, the real estate dealer who has only one idea—and that is to "put it over." Keep clear of this sort until you have found what you wish. Unless you can't find it. I have nothing against real estate traffickers in general, mind you, Quite the contrary. Most of them are fine fellows. I should even suggest that you call one in to close up your deal if you are muddle-minded. But they are prone to be equally eloquent over everything. When I am not contemplating a purchase, I like to hear them talk. But when I am, their mastery of the vocabulary stupefies me. An old darky who used to live in the family had a phrase which describes my feeling precisely. She used to say, "Ef yo'-all would jes' say w'at 'tis and then stop, I could recommember. But w'en yo'-all talk so much, you blosterates my haid and you stagnates me."

So—when you are choosing your cabin site, don't let anybody—however well-informed and well-intentioned—"blosterate your haid and stagnate you." take plenty of time to decide just what you want and how far you dare go from that center of gravity—the job. (Above all things, don't trust to hearsay. Go over your prospective land yourself.) Then when you know what you want, stick to it, even though just after you have realized that your soul craves a lake shore, a dear friend comes along with several acres of "virgin timber with a trout stream right through it, old son." Many people are swept away by the enthusiastic preferences of others.

The best advice for a potential cabin builder is to know your site well. Don't be in a hurry with your new property: plan wisely for its future use. Plans made in haste or without adequate concern for the site, its geography, and weather can form the foundation of many future problems.

Today a site can be altered in ways unavailable to Aldrich. His work was gauged to hand effort and simple techniques that could be accomplished in remote locations without special equipment. Nowadays even a site handicapped by sheer rock bluffs or hampered by boggy soils can be utilized, if you have enough money or sufficient disregard for the environment. Keep in mind, however, that some site limitations, such as poor drainage, often can't be cured entirely.

In general, Aldrich selected good spots for his cabins, although he often failed to give his buildings enough elevation. Placing the wood or log too close to the ground creates a perpetual problem with water damage, rot, or insect invasion. You can correct such flaws by diverting runoff or by replacing damaged portions, but clearly your cabin will be more enjoyable if you are not forever wrestling with nature over faults that could have been avoided. In most cases Aldrich's errors were the result of his aesthetic desire to keep the cabins low and cozy, unimposing and close to the earth. At first, with new and sound logs, the clearance between the lowest log and the ground was sufficient, though minimal. With time and the natural migration of organic material moving down slope, an accumulation of compost slowly bridged the gap between the bottom log and the earth. The problem is intensified because logs age, check, and fissure in ways that make them more susceptible to damage over time.

The logical cure for a cabin that's too low to the ground is to raise it. If the cabin has a massive stone fireplace, so that raising the cabin is either impractical or impossible, you can terraform the area around the cabin, in effect lowering the ground. Creating a new grade around the cabin requires change to your vegetation. The stately trees you value most may be the first to go. But because people leave their urban environments in order to enjoy nature, including the trees, the trees that overtop the cabin may seem too valuable to lose.

The instinct to preserve them is understandable, but the trees one struggles to save may eventually damage the cabin. Direct damage is easy to foresee when a huge tree is too close to the cabin. The giant spruce that looks so imposing near your cabin in summer is even more imposing when it hurtles earthward during a November gale. A tree can easily destroy a portion of the roof, and branches can puncture additional holes. The worst storms tend to come during those times of year when the cabin is unattended, allowing damage to go unchecked, and when repairs are more difficult to make.

Indirect damage is more subtle but no less serious. People often fail to notice the slow encroachment of vegetation on a cabin. What was once open to circulation breezes and the drying effect of the sun becomes shaded and belly-deep in moisture-retaining greenery. In fact, many cabin owners find "charming" the patches of moss that cling to the lower logs or take hold on the roof. There are many good places for moss, but I don't include cabins on that list. And not only is nature constantly reducing organic material into compost to feed new growth, but also many cabin owners contribute to increased building decay by allowing dead leaves to accumulate around the structure, adding fuel to speed decomposition of their logs. To the molds and spores that thrive in piles of rotting leaf debris, your sill log, resting almost on the ground, is as good a candidate for becoming compost as any log fallen in the forest. Even worse, owners sometimes decorate a cabin in ivy or with flower beds raised around the foundation. Structural problems can arise when wood isn't given sufficient protection from those natural forces that foster rot. For years the lower woodwork will appear unchanged. The ants,

I was almost guilty of admitting a fine chap into the sacred precincts of Pals' Cove because he was completely hypnotized by the majesty of the crags and the limitless view over the sparkling "Gitchi Gammi"—as the Ojibways named it to the old Voyageurs. Suddenly I discovered that, above all things, he loved a sunrise swim before breakfast. Now—except for a precious few days of each July and August—if anybody ever tried a sunrise swim in the waters that creep in during the night from the legendary hidden ice fields of old Superior, he probably never ate any more breakfasts. So we wafted our charming friend away to the shores of an inland lake. And instead of a home upon a stern and rock-bound coast, he happily selected several acres lying cozily near civilization and has cut them up into sophisticated fifty-foot lots.

Like most other things in life, any site you may choose will lack some element that your ideal has held. That is, if you have held a very definite ideal of perfection. The more people you have to consider in selecting your site, the more difficult it will be to suit them all. If you are fortunate enough to have youngsters to look out for—they must needs be your first consideration. In that case the overworked and underheeded motto—Safety First. If you are going to suit yourself alone and doggone the rest of the world, your job is comparatively easy.

In our case, as we poked the nose of our canoe about the lake and timber country of the North, Little Pal had both ears pricked up for my comments—in the thought that some day we should be tired of cruising about and want a regular home somewhere in the wilds. She declares that during that six thousand mile travel every time we came to a particularly beautiful spot—rugged with rocks and embroidered in moss—with evergreens walking solemnly side by side through a valley and up a hillside, I would call attention to it joyously with the remark: "Isn't that great? Just like the North Shore of Lake Superior where I used to trout-fish before I knew you!" From which—by a process of feminine deduction—she decided that, when we had our permanent home, it should be on the North Shore of Lake Superior. One year she carelessly suggested we go there on a camping trip instead of canoeing.

So—we took the good ship America out of Duluth, gorged delicious white fish at mealtime, and in darkness piled all our camping duffle off at the small fishing hamlet that was familiar to me. Next morning we hired a gas-boat and cruised miles along shore until we saw a place which seemed to us too good to be true—with its austere rocky headlands enclosing a beautiful friendly cove. Its stretch of pebbly beach was backed by a wall of impenetrable forest green. The air was sweet with wild roses and balsam fragrance.

There we pitched our camp—and there in another year Trailsyde Cabin stood as token of the fact that we believed in love for first site.

First of all, then, choose a site that gives you a thrill.

However, in the romantic surges that sway your bosom just after you have decided to dwell in a log cabin, don't forget that there are extremely prosaic matters to consider. Wood—water—food. The most important practical point, therefore, in selecting a site is to have it within comfortable reach of pure drinking water. Unfortunately, one cannot determine whether or no the water is pure merely by looking at it. (Nor from the taste, alas!)

If there is the slightest doubt about it, have a chemist analyze it for you. It costs little. In fact, your state university will probably be delighted to do it for nothing.

During the period of doubt—boil the water.

Choose a site that gives you a thrill!

however, will notice the difference. So will those spores that thrive in humid shade, such as may be found on the hidden side of a log. By the time the problem is noticed—for example, because something sags—the problem is well advanced.

I remember some people who said there was only one minor problem with their cabin. They had a few carpenter ants in one corner. From their point of view it was a minor inconvenience to sweep up a little sawdust and spray the corner for ants once a week. The slight evidence found inside the cabin, however, was not the issue. When we went outside to see if we could spot further signs, we found little to concern us. A beautiful large rosebush graced the corner of the building. Poking among the roses uncovered no obvious nest of ants. The main body of ants, as is often the case, were located in the central roof beams of the cabin. The inadequately vented attic was an ideal environment where we found ant-made sawdust. The ants had found prime territory: access screened by the rosebush, easy entrance at the corner, and plenty of room to expand in the upper story.

Your cabin site offers other concerns besides the building's adjacent gradient and vegetation, but the closest portion of the site often has the greatest impact on the cabin. Many owners, however, are reluctant to change their immediate vicinity. I can't count the number of times I've told owners about the need to open up the area around a cabin. I point to the buildup of humus, the encroachment of brush, and the potential for wildfire in a cabin surrounded by fuel. But sometimes all the good reasons in the world are insufficient against the weight of sentimentality.

It's true that if you let a cabin become surrounded with dense growth, the idea of clearing it conjures up an image of despoliation. To avoid the shock of a denuded cabing, approach the task in stages. Thin some of the vegetation, remove the worst offenders, tackle the heaviest area of humus accumulation, and contour that area to direct water away from the cabin. Approached gradually, the job is much less offensive, and for every large tree that has to be removed you can substitute a new one. The object, after all, isn't to have a cabin isolated in a sterile field but to develop a practical and attractive setting.

Other features of the cabin's setting cannot be so easily changed. If you build upon a wet spot or a seep, that condition is apt to be with you for-

ever. Likewise, spring runoff is likely to flood the same areas year after year. If the spring thaw puts a torrent at your doorstep, you have a problem that will require much effort to alleviate. Careful study of your property before building will often provide clues to help you avoid problems beforehand or help remedy them later.

When a building is in the wrong place, there is sometimes no solution. In this chapter one of the photos of Aldrich's log cabins has the caption "Glorious—but the front steps sail away!" Oh, if it were only that simple! The steps were merely the first to go. They took several unplanned trips, and the door and sash work facing the lake took at least two unscheduled jaunts as well. But eventually Lake Superior used the porch timbers as a ram to batter down most of the south and east walls. The result was, to say the least, airy.

Next—in ascertaining how far you dare place your cabin from the nearest highway, remember that you will have to ship in supplies somehow if your car cannot get through. Beginning with the necessary building material, which one is compelled to import from civilization. However, if you are a regular he-man with a packsack or have good friends among woodsmen, everything can be packed in settler-wise—even to the cook stove.

Having decided upon your land and consummated its purchase, you will probably pace it over slowly, stopping every few feet with hand shading eyes to aid you in fixing the precise view which will rejoice you as you look out upon it from your cabin. Luckily there will be no one about to report your actions to the nearest alienist. In this way, you will probably discover that your land has many building sites upon it as far as view is concerned. As some of these are likely to be discarded by other folk who are called in to approve your selections, it is just as well to allow a little time in your schedule for adjusting domestic arguments over the precise spot upon which your Dream House is to stand. The length of time thus allotted should vary directly with the number of people whose tastes you consult, and inversely with what you may hear referred to as your own bull-headedness. Bring to bear upon the point—if you would sway any to your notion—that all is not view that matters. Almost any so-called head of the house, if given enough time, ought to be able to think up a sufficient number of arguments which sound important to swing the rest to what is literally his point of view.

Though our widest windows face South because the blue of the lake lies that way and there is a glory of sunlight drifting in through a filigree of green, yet soil and elevation and such practical matters had most to do with the placing of the cabin.

The suggestion to choose a site which is high and dry is likely to bring a smile of tolerant amusement. ("D'ye think we're going to build it in a swamp?") Yet a spot which may be high as the cost of living and dry during Summer and early Fall as the Volstead Act may be partly under water in the Spring. When choosing a lake shore for your site, don't forget that in the season when you are there, it shows it mildest and friendliest aspect. If it is a shallow lake, melting snow and Spring freshets may raise it well over your site. Or, if it be like our own old monster, it may lash itself into such wild fury under pressure of violent storms that it will climb the bank to investigate fifty feet inland. One cabin builder, who loves the great water not wisely but too well, erected his building so far out on a headland that every time there is any storm of sorts it washes all the furniture off his front porch.

After these few observations, one may say with regard to elevation, that all which really matters is to place the cabin enough higher than the surrounding land to be sure of drainage away from the building. In general, the higher you are the better the view—but remember that to build on the highest point may make you victim of the prevailing winds or a brassy sun—and may cause you to have some difficulty about water supply.

Of course, you will choose to dwell among trees—probably among evergreens. Keep in mind that balsams are more lightly rooted than sister spruce and more likely to drop athwart your beloved cabin in violent winds. Maple, oak and large healthy birch are staunch, and white pines a bodyguard. Some trees will have to be cleared out for your building, but in doing this, leave your choicest ones in groups, for trees, like humans, seem to thrive better with a few well-selected comrades to grow alongside. Sound trees, well-rooted and in friendly groups, will withstand all save fire.

Fire is a hazard, but—except in a vast expanse of forest area—a large clearing is not necessary. The settler's cabin is invariably the center of hideous desolation. To the pioneer type of mind, ruthlessness is a mark

Glorious—but the front steps sail away!

of his strength, and love of beauty is a criminal weakness. I still sicken with the memory of a grove of hundred year old cedars that a certain neighbor sacrificed to some vagrant fancy for clearing. Once in a while I wish Nature were animate enough to tell impertinent Man what she really thinks about his smug, spry little decisions!

As to the soil, there is a Biblical precedent for not building upon yielding ground or shifting sands. (Unless you are going to have a basement.) The cabin must be builded upon rock—in fact, upon several rocks whose base is firmly fixed in firm soil foundations. Upon these the sill logs may be laid to hold the floor joists with every confidence that they will be as solid as American currency. Of the large house with a basement—more anon.

It all comes to this: Use your common sense and see your dream cabin clearly in imagination before a stake is placed—for a man is judged by his site. Recently a practical man of affairs disputed this with me and, as his best argument, instanced the site of his own summer home—a rather pretentious affair upon a large acreage. Of course, I had to accept in silence, for how in the world could I tell him that I learned to know him intimately from his choice of site? I had discovered his garage placed upon the point of vantage—commanding a view of hills upon hills rolling away into blue distance—a stream like a silver ribbon flung upon misty green meadows; His house had two views—the dusty highway on one side and the barn upon the other.

However—don't think that I urge you to overlook practical details. By no means. A perfect summer can be ruined by having to carry water half a mile to the house—for by that time little water is left anyhow. Make everything as easy as possible. Don't get lumbago in your back-to-nature!

It is best to establish a trail to the cabin site early in the game—else all growing things may be trampled to death and your woodsy carpet is given the appearance of a logging camp drag-road.

Not only your local aids in construction but the oft-mentioned relatives and friends are more than likely to be anxious to improve on Nature. One member of your household will decide that she will have a rockery—here—precisely where her foot is planted—and forthwith begins to gather up and scatter all over the place all the "pretty stones" she can find. Another, in the inspiration of making a hanging basket—which will never materialize, by the way—bears off a large chunk of velvety moss from the rock where it has grown for the last fifty years, and yanks up little trailing vines that wave helpless tendrilly pink roots in the air in mute protest.

It is hopeless to try to impress some people with the idea that no one can ever really own anything of living Nature. At most, we have but a temporary stewardship over it. I once saw a perfectly sane man, in sheer exuberance at considering himself master of all he surveyed, deliberately kick to pieces an exquisite mossy mound upon which grew tiny forest flowers wherein were fairies curled up sound asleep. So gorged was he with possessorship that he did not even hear their cries of terror and rage as they fled hither and yon, bearing with them the sad tidings that moonlight parties were over for the season. Their loveliest ballroom had been wantonly destroyed.

Now—before you decide to be ruthless about any of your property—just because it is yours in a legal sort of way—why not do as the birds do and live amid your surroundings for a while before making a change? It may be that the very tree whose removal you determined

upon before you came to comrade with it, will be to you a friendly tree with healing in its leaves. If not—it takes but a moment to sweep it from the landscape—an infinitesimal fraction of the time it took it to grow there.

Until your cabin is set in place, it is impossible for even the most zealously imaginative to picture it precisely enough to be able to landscape satisfactorily. Moreover, be your cabin small or large, it will be sure to have about it scattered chips from log fittings. You are not going to have a brilliant success with landscaping until you have your workmen, and the souvenirs they have left of their visit, out of the way.

One suggestion I might make with regard to the gentle restraint of aforesaid workmen. Unless you have a Nature enthusiast as superintendent of your building, it is not a bad idea to rope off certain sections of your ground which you are particularly anxious not to have trampled down by the sturdy boots of your crew. Their intentions are good, but they make your forest look like the place that is paved with 'em.

Live among your surroundings for a while.

CHAPTER THREE

WHAT IS A "PIONEER CABIN"?

Two things now are decided upon. The site and the fact that you are building of logs. For one may assume surely, that you are building of logs?

There are other types of vacation homes. There is the board cottage which can be made convenient and even artistic. In fact, when a man insists on boards it demonstrates pretty clearly that he hasn't a soul for logs. Although there may be other reasons for his decision, not esthetic but financial—anyhow, we design him a clapboard cottage and question him no further.

Another material that has been long favored for vacation homes is the weathered shingle. Now shingles are all right at a summer resort—or in fact any place where you have to wear a necktie to dinner to please your wife—but in the forest primeval I feel like the old logger who ran across such a construction one day and opined that it "must of taken a dog-goned long time for a feller to whittle all them chips off'n a log." In a forest environment there is only one material to use. A log cabin has the Topsylike aspect of having "jest growed."

Moreover, consider the record of log cabins in this country. What a part they have played in history. Did you ever stop to think that the reason we have so few great men nowadays is because there are so few log cabins for them to be born in? In order to insure its future place in history the slogan of this country ought to be "Back to Log Cabins!"

Then see what would happen.

But right in this connection, let me dampen your enthusiasm over gathering up all the architectural books on the pioneer cabin. If you are

Aldrich uses a sketch of the replica of a pioneer cabin that formerly was on display in the Minnesota Historical Society. In chapter 14 Aldrich says that he built the replica shown in the sketch, which he reproduced three times in his book. The replica itself was disassembled and put into storage, and when last I checked, the Historical Society was uncertain what had become of it.

Aldrich's replica of a pioneer cabin seems more romantic than historically accurate. The little building seems to me an idealized version of pioneer life rather than a portrayal of what people actually required for survival in undeveloped territory. In Aldrich's era the image of a snug and cozy little cabin was commonly accepted by a public eager for a comforting view of the past. In reality most pioneers lived in mere shacks that were surrounded by various sheds and outbuildings. Housing, as Aldrich himself suggests, took second place to animal barns. On Lake Superior shores where farming was relatively impractical, the fish house received more attention than the family home. Indeed, the first house built on a property was often considered expendable, although the family might live in it for decades before building the "real house." You can still find a few of these relics quietly falling into disrepair while the nearby "real house" dominates the scene.

Despite the romantic tendencies of his era, Aldrich conscientiously presents some buildings actually used by pioneering settlers. One example has a steep roof. Before the easy availability of rolled roofing materials, the best device for keeping the interior dry was a steep roof to shed water

quickly. Building a steeply pitched roof requires considerable skill and experience, and it usually requires a practiced team of experienced people. Easy-to-build low-pitched roofs became practical with the use of tar products. Tar paper had a vast impact on how people built. Rolled roofing suited Aldrich's picturesque image of a cabin nestled low to the ground. And a low structure is easier to build because you don't have to wrestle heavy materials as high off the ground. The new materials, then, made building a cabin more of a do-it-yourself project.

The architectural and recreational ideal of a rustic cabin was an enormous departure from the previous ideal of a summer home, the highly urbanized house in rural surroundings. Aldrich rejected those elaborate summer homes of the gentry who packed off family and servants for an entire summer in the countryside. Aldrich's inspiration had a different origin.

A drawing shows what is apparently an unused Lake Superior fish house. The roof has an easy-to-build moderate pitch but seems to show rather advanced decay, which developed rapidly when a roof of that sort was left unattended. It's unfortuante that Aldrich doesn't provide more information here. Perhaps he was impressed by the formidable number of purlin logs supporting the vertical roof boards. The log work may have been of quite good quality, but the inadequate roof placed the entire structure in jeopardy. It is, however, somewhat confusing to compare a seasonal utility building with a log cabin intended for continual habitation.

The following drawing shows a hewn log home in Hovland near where Aldrich built his cabins. The steep roof on the front would rapidly shed snow or rain. But note that such a design was impractical for a wider span, which would require truss work and long tie logs: the task was beyond the means or work force of a typical settler family. Most early log houses were similar to this one. The initial structure was often a single room of modest size, with a steep roof and attic loft. Additional rooms were added at the gable ends because the eaves walls were too low for expansion. In this picture we can see the advent of tar-paper roofings: the last addition has a low-pitched roof. Rarely did a cabin rise to one-and-a-half or two stories with an option for adding on at either gable or eaves walls. As the saltbox shape on the east coast grew from a particular pattern of adding on, so the pattern in the rural north was the ram-

going to be a pioneer, you are going to wear your pioneership, as the plaintive, lovelorn maid wore her rue, "with a difference." This difference has its rise in a present day sense of freedom. Remember that our forebears utilized logs because they had no other choice. We utilize logs because they are our first choice. Pioneering has become an art instead of a duty. Study pioneer cabins all you want to—it will be an interesting dip into evolution, for however beautiful they are, you will find an air of grim taciturnity and gritted teeth about the homes of our forefathers which suggests a child set upon a stool and told to work her sampler. They are quaint—but aren't they a bit severe and unhappy about it? Haven't they a sort of all-work-and-no-play puritanism about 'em?

We are beginning to find out that a thing is not beautiful merely because it is old. It would be a sad commentary on human progress if this were true. Nor is a thing inherently lovely because it is modern art. Balance—proportion—a certain symmetry—these are the fundamentals of beauty. Different ages have striven differently to approach these ideals of art—which remain austerely unchangeable. Where the efforts of our forebears were successful, they are worth emulating. Where they failed, we read a lesson and strive differently. I stress this point a bit for, in my work, I am constantly assailed with the insistence: "I want a real old-time log cabin."

Pioneer cabin in Minnesota Historical Society rooms.

Yet if you gave these clients certain types of the "real old-time cabin," you would certainly lose your client—and any other who saw your attempt to follow this sole specification. There are occasional instances of a real artist at work upon an old-time masterpiece, but isn't it usually the beautiful handiwork of Father Time—and not of Grandfather Puritan—which is the real attraction of the picturesque pioneer cabin?

Seldom does one come across a modern settler's log shack that is not constructed with a rank disregard of an intrinsic beauty in the logs themselves and what may be wrought of them. Casting our lot among fisher folk and "newcomer" homesteaders, we have had ample opportunity to study the modern pioneer at close range. Oddly enough, though accustomed in his own native land to the beauty of stalwart, hand-wrought fashionings, the immigrant seems to despise the charm of sincere and thorough-going workmanship as soon as he sets foot upon our shores. He holds as his ideal from the first a better knock-down house than his cousin's who came over four years earlier—enclosing a larger brass bed than his uncle's—and a shinier golden oak dining room table than his nephew's. To meet the cost of these, he utilizes the "shack" for which he constantly apologizes—as he patches it up twice a year, clapping on a board here and there over the logs to conceal poor workmanship, adding various lean-to effects as his family or his live stock increases. In every line of the hill-roofed walls with their logs ill-matched and ill-fitted, sloppily chinked and calked, is inscribed the legend, "We hate this thing, but it's got to do for us until we can afford a factory-made house."

As great amaze as I've ever seen upon a human countenance appeared upon the face of a Norwegian homesteader when he discovered that a regular he-man would build a log cabin when he could afford something else—and that such a building could actually be beautiful.

So—what the phrase "pioneer cabin" undoubtedly means in the mind of the person who glibly tosses it off—feeling that therewith he has set forth every detail for your help—is that he desires a home which looks as if it were one piece with its forest setting. One which does not flaunt its newness. One which suggests comfort and the mellow joy of living. One in which the modern concessions to convenience are skillfully hidden—if, indeed, they are present at all.

To hurdle another misapprehension before we go any further, there seems to be an idea that because logs grow on trees a log cabin is the most inexpensive building one can attempt in the woods. This is, in

bling structure shown here. Limitations in manpower and materials forced many homesteads to grow end-to-end, like railcars. Most of that early construction is long gone, replaced by better housing.

The log shack that Aldrich shows next is a lean-to. Set directly on the ground and covered by a nearly horizontal and consequently leaky roof, such a structure provided a minimum of protection while requiring a minimum of effort to build. Most lean-tos were only used seasonally, such as for fall hunting. Few of these humble little shacks have survived the years, and we see them today mostly in old photographs.

Picturesque but—

In reading Aldrich's comments about homesteaders and their sloppily built cabins, one must consider the social climate of the time. As a successful architect from the city, Aldrich possibly forgot that these people, whom he criticizes for taking so little care with their log buildings, seldom had much cash. Their primary occupation was survival, and they were striving to move up to housing built of sawmill and factory materials, such as Aldrich enjoyed three quarters of the year in Minneapolis.

With a board clapped on here and there.

The frame-building designs Aldrich includes are unimpressive by today's standards. Although they have little to do with log construction, I have retained them because they reflect design characteristics of that time. They show some typical Aldrich touches, struggling to be cozily close to the earth and yet large enough to be useful. For example, his Nautilus design uses a dogleg roofline to gain space without requiring a taller, more massive roof.

Many buildings from the Aldrich era, shortly after the First World War, are still with us today because that period saw the first major expansion of summer cottages and cabins for the middle and upper-middle classes. Those cabins conformed to the current styles and available materials. Remodeling or refurbishing them now could demand elaborate solutions to overcome the limitations of low building height and roofs with

general, untrue. Remember logs are potential lumber. If you are purchasing your logs, the man from whom you buy them makes you a price which varies according to the amount he thinks he can get for them from somebody else who has a sawmill or—alackaday!—a pulp mill. (I never pass a news stand flamboyant with magazines—about three of which are worth wasting time upon—without an inward apology to the trees for such abasement.)

If you have enough logs on your own place to build your cabin, your problem of expense is reduced—but even then, to construct properly fitted log work takes slow, patient labor. Labor costs money. The price of it varies with the demand for it in the part of the country in which you build. Labor union price does not, of course, affect the casual axman or native carpenter. Work is, indeed, often a godsend in places where a "living wage" is lower than in the cities. When this fellow has his planting done, and that fellow has his pulpwood cut, and the other fellow's team is doing nothing but eating its head off in the pasture, labor can be had for much less per hour than the city artisan demands. But remember that it takes much longer to fit a log properly than it does to nail a board into place.

Hard upon my amazed discovery that many lovers of the lake and forest and stream and mountain were selecting logs simply because they thought that would be the easiest, quickest and cheapest way to put up a summer home came my realization that one ought not to destroy this illusion without having something constructive to offer. It's no fun seeing a grieved and disappointed shadow in the eyes of one who comes to you eager and enthusiastic about his vacation home. Nor does one derive any great pleasure as one travels about from the sight of out-of-proportion, ill built, tag end board shacks in a beautiful—and helpless—setting.

For that reason it seemed wise to design a few substitute cottages, to offer clients who find logs too expensive, in which grace of line and beauty of construction is not lost by reason of lack of professional assistance. No accredited architect is going to bother with a little lake cottage to cost, complete, less than five hundred dollars, for instance. His education has been too expensive, his more remunerative clients too insistent upon the work he is doing for them. But it seems a doggone shame that a fellow can't have beauty instead of ugliness—at the same price. A roof line may make the difference to a regular person between the forest home he (or more particularly "she") wants and a "shack" to be endured rather than loved.

The designs, "Avon," "Bard," "Cross" and "Dream"—shown elsewhere—are all "one room and porch" cottages, and these can be built—with lumber prices as they are at present—for from three to five hundred dollars. "Eden," three rooms and porch, and "Nautilus," (in its first, or two-room-and-porch stage) can be built for about seven hundred dollars. As a rough estimate—very rough—the cost of these same designs if developed in logs, with the proper fittings and excellent ax work, would be about double. Slipshod workmanship and sub-standard materials, remember, do not make a cottage any cheaper. They merely make it look cheaper. Costs given with these designs are the lowest consistent with sound construction and standard materials. Don't pride yourself on being sport enough to endure ramshackle-ism. The "Red Gods" are no more constant "callers" because the roof is leaky or the lumber worm eaten or the glass in the windows opaque.

insufficient pitch. Also, many people today look upon their summer cabins as potential retirement homes, and the shift in function often requires considerable work and expense.

Settler's log shack

"Eden" has three rooms.

"AVON"

"CROSS"

"BARD"

"DREAM"

Good lines may be had with boards.   One-room-and-porch cottages.

CHAPTER FOUR

CHOOSING YOUR TYPE OF CABIN

There's a double-barreled question I put to the prospective client who comes a-roving to my door:

"How much to invest and how many to accommodate?"

Sometimes he knows the one definitely, sometimes he knows the other. Seldom both. Often neither.

After this is given satisfactory reply, the next thing is to make up your mind—and the minds of your family and the friends you expect to bid to your forest sanctuary—just how rough you wish your "roughing it" to be. In a 15x18 one-room cabin can be comfortably accommodated all of the living necessities for four people. But the people must be congenial, have good dispositions, and not snore.

On the other hand, there are those who would demand four separate sleeping rooms—with baths, lights, heating plant, garage, and servants' quarters. Probably somewhere between these two lie your requirements.

The main thing is to determine precisely what you need for your comfort. Make a list of the things you can't be happy without. Don't set the price you are willing to put into a woodland home so that it approaches the vanishing point and then demand all the conveniences of urban life. Remember that it costs a lot more to take a bath in the woods than it does in the city—unless you utilize the bath tubs Mother Nature has put there.

When you have made a list of the items that you regard as absolutely necessary for your comfort, consider it carefully and see if you can't cut it down one-third. Ask yourself if, after all, your grandfather's sturdiness and the awesome age to which your great-grandfather lived were not

Aldrich began his log cabin career with his own cabin, Trailsyde, in Hovland. It still exists but not in its original form. The first changes were made by Aldrich himself when he became dissatisfied with the limitations of a one-room cabin.

It's impossible to determine which changes Aldrich made first, but one of them must have been extending the chimney to achieve a better draw. Apparently his original fireplace smoked. It's only my guess that Aldrich tackled a balky fireplace first, but if you've ever spent any time trapped in a room dominated by a smoking beast of a fireplace, you'll agree that a fireplace constantly billowing smoke inside is a fireplace destined to be either unused or repaired. Aldrich also added a copper smoke lip to the fireplace mouth. Aldrich was rediscovering the ratios and features of Count Rumford's fireplace specifications of an earlier century.

Another addition to Trailsyde was a skylight that could be opened on the north side across from the fireplace. At first Aldrich connected a rope-and-pulley arrangement to a tree, and later he devised a simple method of opening and closing the skylight from inside. As well as letting in more light, the skylight acted as a vent to help clear the upper air, allowing stray smoke to escape. Despite remedial improvements, a faulty fireplace will never work quite right, especially on gusty days or when the flue is cold.

Small windows, approximately one foot square, were added in the east and west walls near the north corners. These windows let fresh air into the lower bunks on each side of the cabin. The interior must have often

been hazy with smoke to require such measures: he cut these windows only in his own cabin with its balky fireplace.

From the outset Aldrich probably had to adjust his plan to make his single-room cabin useful and pleasant. The two double bunks on either side of the room might do for guests for a while, but the cabin was both cramped and lacking in privacy. Aldrich removed the little stoop porch with a projecting overhang and replaced it with a full screened porch along the entire north wall, an eave wall. Because of the low eaves, the porch ran out of headroom before reaching a room of useful width. To compensate, Aldrich deliberately tilted the floor in order to gain two precious inches of headroom. The pronounced slope of the porch floor, two inches in eight feet, required special cuts for all the vertical members. Even with that much tinkering, the porch roof was almost horizontal, and the porch was anything but spacious.

The porch had other problems. For some reason, Aldrich decided on two exterior doors, north and west. With the interior door to the cabin proper, Aldrich's little porch was broken up by three doorways, which is simply one too many. The visible signs of use, however, show that the porch was an essential addition to the cabin. It provided space for storage, a four-foot square table, two chairs, several shelves, and a bed protected from the elements by roll-down canvas curtains.

When I came upon the scene nearly sixty years later, the original slope of the porch floor had become steeper because several inches of the bottom support log had rotted into the earth. The one benefit was an increased slope of the roof. Over the years, however, the roof had suffered from heavy snow loads and was swayed and damaged. Using external supports to hold in place the roof with its log rafters, I demolished the rotten walls and floor. The new floor is supported by treated lumber set on concrete pads. It matches exactly the size of the original, but it is not sloped. The rim is triple plated, and the joists are set on twelve-inch centers, doubled up for three joists on either side of the center. The floor frame of two-by-six lumber is far stronger than the original.

The rebuilt porch copies the original in size. The west door is precisely where Aldrich had it, right down to the last dimension. I eliminated the second exterior porch door because it sacrificed too much space and had weakened the top plates in the wall. I installed windows that open, in

due—in part at least—to the things they didn't have.

By the time I have gone at my clients this way, they usually demand—with considerable show of reason, I will admit:

"Can't I have what I want?"

There is one answer to this, "You can have anything in the world you want—if you are sure you want it and can pay for it." No architect, however, is a magician. He cannot wave a wand and bring up a ten thousand dollar cabin when you authorize him to design one that will come within your figure of twenty-five hundred. A conscientious architect, with experience to guide him, can tell you very nearly what your building is going to cost as soon as you tell him what you wish. If that cost is beyond you, he will, with considerable waste of time to himself, go over your ideas with you and tell you frankly what you must sacrifice to have it come within reach of your appropriation.

"Trailsyde" is cozy in hunting season.

This is the proverbial quandary of the architect. He is often placed in the position of making something out of nothing. However, the designer of homes for hours of ease—the out-of-door architect (if indeed there be any of the profession plain fool enough to follow the fullness of his heart instead of the emptiness of his purse) probably has the most amusing experiences with those ignorant of the cost of such ease. A sweet little soul, with a longing to commune with Nature, brings me what's left over from the house-money for a month and wishes a three thousand dollar cabin for it.

During an exhibition of models made to scale—half inch to the foot, completely constructed and furnished—a dear little old lady approached me and heartened me with an offer to buy one of them for a couple of dollars rather than have me throw them away, she said, after the exhibit was over. Her little grandson would like one for a bird house.

So—having made up your mind that there will be a reasonable congeniality between the "how much" and "how many" in your case, let us begin (as we ourselves began) with a single small cabin "for self and guests"—determining on the unit plan of increase in size. Our group of units now consists of "Trailsyde," the original one-room cabin; "The

place of the screens and canvas curtains. The exterior detailing is less elaborate now. I stayed as close to the original as I could, while eliminating the major faults. I felt that a more conventional exterior was appropriate to the transition from screened porch to closed porch.

From the fireplace and porch on Trailsyde, Aldrich learned to avoid mistakes on later cabins. He never again tried to squeeze in a porch that hadn't been part of the original plan. And no other porch had more than one outside door. The porches he designed for other cabins, whether open or merely screened, were connected to the cabin itself by French doors that admitted daylight into the interior room.

The photo of a large interior with fireplace and table is of Trailsyde. The hazy central area may be the result of the light, but the fireplace, shown here before the addition of the smoke lip, is probably the culprit. The ends of the bunks, supported by birch poles, are seen on either side. For privacy the bunks were curtained off at night. The plate shelf above the left window was later given a mate over the right window, and later still the cooking area was expanded to fill in the corner. The single room was, as you imagine, quite full.

One room may contain all comforts.

The interior view shown in the photo is almost the same today. Fortunately, much of the original furniture has been saved. While cleaning the interior, I could locate exactly where objects had been, and I returned them to their original places. Over the years, of course, the interior was gradually changed, but if Aldrich were to walk in today, he'd find it very much as he left it.

Aldrich eventually built a one-room guest cabin, called the Roost, about a hundred feet from Trailsyde. The photo shows the northeast corner of the Roost. There was another bed in the northwest corner. The south wall had large windows with a good view of the lake. The room also held a small table, some chairs, a wardrobe, and a heating stove. An open L-shaped porch was eventually enlarged, added to the gable end.

Roost," our guest cabin; "Crow's Nest," atop a cliff—a studio which may be used for guests in time of dire need—and a Workshop for making furniture and tinkering with the hundred and one things with which a man likes to fool away time when he has it to fool away. (When friends ask us what in the world we find to do during the two to five months we spend in the woods, there is only one reply: there's always so much to do that we haven't time to do anything.)

"Totem Pole Lodge" includes four rooms and porch.

Of course, you are going to inquire first off if it is not much more expensive to build separate buildings than an all-in-one. No—not much more. The advantage is that it is not necessary to build all of them at once. The unit plan may be utilized in many ways as your family and needs increase. Cooking and eating may be separated from sleeping and assembly quarters; or the "bunk house" may be separate, the living room and kitchen in one—utilizing the living room as a dining room at meal-time. If you plan to build one unit the first year and add another when you are ready, the two-division unit, living room and kitchen, would be ample for comfort, with bunks in the living room or on the porch for sleeping quarters the first year.

How about having it all eventually under one roof, you ask, adding rooms as needed, instead of separate buildings? If you work to a plan in this scheme there is not much disadvantage except that even with careful oiling your logs of last year are not going to be precisely the same shade of mellowness as this year's. For a year or two, there will be no disguising the fact that your house is built on the installment plan. Time, however, covers a multitude of sins. But if you have decided on this Nautilus type of house, have your plans for the final and complete home drawn before you lay a log. Don't try to add a shed roof here and a lean-to there and a gable end on the other—as the spirit moves you—and expect your place to look like anything but your grandmother's crazy quilt.

"The Roost" is a one-room guest cabin.

Around that time, Aldrich build the Crow's Nest for his wife. Elsewhere in the book there is a photo of her writing at a little desk in the southeast corner of Trailsyde. Now the Crow's Nest became her writing retreat. At ten feet by eight feet, the Crow's Nest is tiny indeed, but it gave her the quiet she needed to pursue her career. With the excellent little fireplace blazing in the Crow's Nest, the atmosphere must have been almost too soothing to stimulate a writer! Set apart on a crag, the Crow's Nest is in a world of its own.

With separate buildings for his wife and guests, Aldrich enlarged his space without having to add rooms to Trailsyde, a task that would have presented enormous practical and aesthetic problems for a building never designed to grow. Trailsyde was left mostly as first imagined, an enlarged version of the idealized pioneer cabin.

Aldrich's approach was gradually evolving, as in the drawing and floor plan of a one-room cabin in this chapter. The sketch shows a somewhat longer cabin than Trailsyde, affording one window a clear view past the porch. In this instance Aldrich placed the fireplace in the north wall and the porch on the south and west walls (I am assuming that the uphill side is north). As usual, the north wall appears too low to the ground. This proposed building is a more practical version of Trailsyde, slightly larger and turned round.

Also shown in this chapter are Totem Pole Lodge and Seven Glens, both built near Trailsyde for customers who wanted better rustic accommodations with more than a single room. On each of these Aldrich did considerably better work than he did on his first cabin. His log-fitting skills remained somewhat weak, but the designs improved, along with his use of fixtures and appointments.

The model of Seven Glens shown in the photo is very close to the actual cabin, although there are a few clear differences. The door on the far right is a screen door off the porch, which would be downslope, facing the lake. The door of solid wood, at the bottom of the picture, opens onto a room of indeterminate purpose. A window is centered on the south wall, and large closets flank the window and create an interior bay or possibly a breakfast nook. A medicine cabinet has been built into this room. With the back half of the fireplace partly in the room, along with two more doors to the kitchen and the living room, the space is cut up, leaving no practical area for a bed or much furniture.

The Seven Glens kitchen, on the left side, is almost the same size, except for a costly and useless jog in the log wall. The kitchen also has three doors, one into the living room alongside the fireplace, one into the adjoining room across the back of the fireplace, and one outdoors where the lean-to wall juts out from the living-room wall. Again the number

"Seven Glens"—Interior.

In balancing the advantages and disadvantages of the unit and all-in-one type, there are several things to consider. In the first place—how sociable are you? If, like Sir Joseph Porter, you are "seeking the seclusion that a cabin grants," you probably will be happier if that is not shared by your sisters and your cousins and your aunts. Some people's idea of a perfect vacation is to have the world and his wife with them every single minute chattering into their ears. They adore the fashion of shouting back and forth until midnight, through—or over—thin partitions and have no reticences about revelatory sounds. If this is the sort of person you are, have an all-in-one with board partitions halfway up to the ceiling—but make your own plans. This book is not for you.

There are, however, disadvantages in the unit plan which the all-in-one does not have. First of all, if you propose having your guests take meals with you, it sometimes means that they will have to face a driving rain in order to scramble over to the cabin where the feast is prepared.

Model of "Seven Glens."

But—to offset that—never have guests who are not good sports. Again in the case of the one-room unit, it is difficult to find a proper time or place to take a bath. Even making a change in the attire has its problems, with the guests gathered hilariously around the open fire. Even in a one-room affair, however, a division for washing and dressing can be managed by curtain or screen. Moreoever, many of the conventions are slack in living the wild life. One of our most conventional guests managed to stand everything but brushing her teeth out-of-doors. That was too much. Each soul has its special pet inhibitions.

The one-room unit, however, is only one phase of the so-called unit plan. Although the main cabin may have enough rooms to accommodate the entire family, a separate cabin for guests—or servants if you must have them cluttering up your vacation—is desirable. Presumably your guests will like the seclusion of their own special abode quite as well as you will like having your own privacy at times. In general, those who seek out log cabins in the woods instead of fashionable resorts feel the need of relaxation and rest from the usual amenities of the world. Through our actual experience, we have discovered that our guests were joyously grateful for their unaccustomed independence in a cabin all their own. "The Roost" is fitted with all the necessaries of light housekeeping, so that if those who have come to us for rest do not care to arise and breakfast with the family, they may get their own breakfast at any time they choose. It is surprising how many rifts in the enjoyment of the day this arrangement smooths out for both host and guest. Few people are at their best, dispositionally, in the early morning. Of course, in the case of a "singleton" guest, especially of the feminine gender, it is perhaps wiser to take her under the shelter of the main roof. Hence it is well to be prepared in your unit plan with an extra couch on the porch, or a day-bed in the living room—or even, perchance, an upper bunk for storing a timid and non-snoring guest. The youngsters, by the way, will be tickled pink with a tent having a board floor which is a permanent fixture.

of doors cuts up the space rather badly, although at least these doors are close together. (Older wooden buildings often have many more doors than seem practical, and some old houses have an outside door for virtually every room. The fear of fire caused many people to want to always be near an exit.) Kitchen cabinets run along the wall at the bottom of the picture and part way up the left. A flue for a wood-burning kitchen range was provided in the back wall of the fireplace, and a stove in the adjoining room required another flue, rendering the Seven Glens fireplace massive and complicated with a total of three chimney flues. The kitchen has one of a matching pair of double-sided cabinets situated on either side of the fireplace. The exterior kitchen door is a Dutch door, much favored by Aldrich to prevent cool air from entering at floor level. Unfortunately, the entire north kitchen wall, on the left side of the picture, is too low to the ground, as is the rest of the north wall with its slight projection for built-in cabinetry, showing in the roofline of the model. On the whole, this kitchen is reasonably practical and useful.

The living room is large and open. The fireplace, with matching cabinets and doors on both sides, is attractive. The arch, at the top of the picture, frames an alcove for two small beds foot-to-foot or furniture for seating. Given the lack of sleeping space in the cabin otherwise, I think Aldrich intended the main room to be also used for sleeping, as is suggested by the deep matching closets on both sides of the arch. There is a tiny bed-sized loft above the arch. In Aldrich's model the arched area is closed off. In the actual cabin the loft was left open for easier access to the single spring and mattress.

Seven Glens is heavily favored with matching pairs of cabinets, cupboards, closets, and wrought fixtures for candles. The matching units on both sides of the fireplace are the most successful in aesthetic appeal. The others vary in utility as well as aesthetics, but they provide ample closed storage in a cabin that might otherwise look unattractive by day, if all the bedding had to be left in the open. No doubt his experience in the one room of Trailsyde prompted Aldrich to devise remedies for clutter.

The porch at Seven Glens shows how Aldrich struggled to retain the aesthetics of a simple cabin while gaining interior room. For example, he improved the arrangement of the doors. The biggest change from the Trailsyde design was to place the Seven Glens porch on the downslope side of the cabin. At Trailsyde the options for size and roof pitch were limited because that porch was fighting an uphill grade, a problem Aldrich avoided in later designs. The Seven Glens porch has a few steps down from the living room. By using the lay of the land to his advantage, Aldrich gained headroom for a suitable porch without having to flatten his roofline too much. The result is a more harmonious whole. Of course, when a porch is placed on the downhill side of a cabin, the scenery from the porch will be excellent, but the view from inside will suffer. A partial solution was provided by the French doors that open from the living room onto the porch. Looking through the porch to see outdoors isn't ideal, but it's a reasonable compromise.

From the perspective of today, when cabin use is often extended into spring and fall, the advantages of a screened porch are obviously limited, however. In fact, on the shores of Lake Superior a screened porch is apt to go unused much of the summer. A porch enclosed against the wind is far more practical and comfortable.

Aldrich had a fascination with candles, and he fitted the walls with wrought sconces, especially at Seven Glens and Croixsyde. He does not show the sconces in his book.

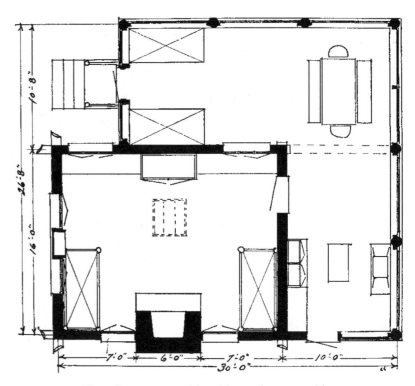

Plan of one-room cabin with porch on two sides.

Interior—"Seven Glens"

A Word About Dimensions

The size of your single cabins—or the rooms of your all-in-one—varies with your purse and the number of the household. It is impossible to give any definite figures to cover all needs. There are, however, certain proportions which are pleasing. A perfectly square building or room is always inartistic and boxy. A one-room cabin 16x20 is a convenient size for a family of two to four and the same dimensions in the living room of a larger cabin will be found satisfactory.

In our 11x14 guest cabin are cheerfully accommodated two single bunks—end to end—small cook stove, a table and chairs, dressing-stand and stand with cupboards below for washing one's face or one's dishes. This is the minimum size for such a cabin, however, and requires neat housekeeping. But it is an ideal size for the bedroom of a larger cabin, giving plenty of room for wardrobes and dressing conveniences. Windows placed the long side of the room give an abundance of light and air and add charm always. If you are insisting upon a bathroom, it is best placed between the two bedrooms, of course, or next the kitchen in case of a yearning for hot water. The kitchen of a cabin is usually, for convenience sake, the gathering place for meals if there are not servants. In this event, have it a long room rather than squarish—with the dining end as far away from the stove as possible. Your kitchen end should be large enough to give you plenty of cupboard room with space also for stove and wood box. The ice box is wisely placed as far from heat as possible. In placing your kitchen in plan, you will consider it along with your living-room fireplace (if you are using a wood cook stove) in order that the one chimney will serve both rooms. Of course, with an oil cook stove, this consideration is unnecessary.

These are simply suggestions to aid you in your planning—for nobody but yourself can tell you precisely what you want or how spacious and pretentious a cabin you intend to afford. The number and size of your rooms increase the cost of your forest home proportionately—especially as you are surely going to have none but log partitions for beauty, harmony of design, and the comfort of soundlessness. If I seem to reiterate this matter of taking the edge from noise, it is because no one but a person who has lived in the quiet of the woods realizes how clearly sounds carry and how impossible it is to have the rest for which one has sought if voices, and dishes and screen door bangings—not to enumerate other noises of the household—are eternally clattering about one day and night.

Sketch of one-room cabin.

CHAPTER FIVE

GENERAL DISCUSSION OF LOGS. KINDS AND SIZES
AND LENGTHS

Like charity, your logs should begin at home. Or as near home as possible. If you can find the sort of logs you wish near to your site, it rather goes without saying that they will be much cheaper than if they were hauled in from a distance. Although it would be penny wise and pound foolish, clearly, to denude your place of good timber in order to procure logs for your cabin, it is wise to take proper cognizance of the logs in your immediate vicinity before deciding to pay freight upon

Your logs may begin at home.

In Aldrich's day, for the most part, the log-cabin builder had to use logs available locally. Aldrich's discussion of selecting logs is of less interest to us today because a wide range of natural and milled logs are available from a variety of sources. Your choice of materials is not limited to what's available in your immediate area, and you may select widely according to your tastes and pocketbook.

Aldrich preferred small logs. Indeed, compared to today's cabins of massive logs, Aldrich's cabins appear to be made of sticks. The reasons for using small logs are fairly obvious. Logs of small size are easier to handle: they require a smaller work force and less equipment. Six or seven large logs of twelve-inch diameter will yield a wall of roughly conventional height. Big logs, however, require big efforts to move them, especially in raising them high on the growing wall. As much effort goes into positioning logs as into fitting them. Logs with a four-inch diameter are much easier to move into place, but you have to use three times as many of them to make a wall. That means three times as much fitting, but scribing and fitting logs, though tedious, doesn't require the sort of work force needed for big logs. The early do-it-yourselfer builder had to select a style and material that could be managed at a remote location with limited resources.

Aldrich recommends not mixing log species and not building in stages. He had learned from Trailsyde. In the hunting-season photo of Trailsyde the lighter-colored logs are visible beneath the two closest windows. In this first attempt at building a cabin, he mixed materials found

on the site, and the cabin looks peculiar. Aldrich used wood stain on the interior to even out the color, but many of his logs didn't accept stain very well. Finally, in an attempt, I suspect, to make a virtue of necessity, he deliberately accented some logs. The top, or plate, log upon which his rafters rested was stained a mahogany red hue all around the room, along with the rafters, purlins, and ridge. The logs below the plate log were given a wash of walnut brown stain. Further darkened by soot from his smoking fireplace, Trailsyde became more than a little gloomy inside.

Also, Aldrich recommends using shaved logs, not logs that are only peeled of their bark. Because he didn't shave his own logs for Trailsyde, the sap wood was left intact. The outside of the log had a smooth look, but intact sap wood resists application of stain and varnish. At Trailsyde he had to make repeated applications of stain in order to cover up the drips and streaks that resulted from staining sap wood. In his later cabins Aldrich peeled and shaved his logs, and he did not mix log species.

His admonition about not using sawmill timber for rafters or joists where they might be seen is based entirely on aesthetics, and in this case I wish he'd been as fussy about strength as he was about looks. Some of his rafters were too spindly and frail. They were further weakened as years of drying heat made them increasingly brittle. On some of his roofs, the porch roofs especially, the roof boards are almost more structural than the rafters. A springy roof, if it is not badly decayed from leaks, can be improved by adding a skin of plywood over the boards and then reroofing the whole. Additional purlins or knee braces can likewise help support a sagging roof.

I remedied one Aldrich porch roof by adding a two-by-four rafter on either side of each original pole rafter. I then covered the repair with a ceiling of beaded paneling of the sort used near the turn of the century for ceilings, pantry walls, and the like. The interior effect is satisfactory. From outside, the cabin looks unchanged, with only the pole rafters showing.

It may be better to build an entirely new roof using substantial rafters and a new ridge or scissor trusses to overtop the old roof and create a steeper roofline. Such a device will bring the weight out to the walls,

them and then tote them in from the nearest landing. The price of logs varies in different parts of the country. But when you are haggling with your prospective dealer, make sure that his figure on logs is the price delivered to the site you have chosen. Otherwise you may find that your cost of delivery will exceed the cost of your material.

"What Kind of Logs?"

The sort of timber you select for your building will probably be the sort of timber that you can secure with the least possible expenditure of labor and money. In other words, when a man, wishing to construct a log cabin as reasonably as possible, asks me what kind of logs he shall choose, I counter with the words of the ancient wheeze of the spinster in front of the stamp window: "What kinds have you?"

In our Northern part of the country the reply given is usually "Evergreen." Which means White, Norway and Jack pine, spruce, balsam, and cedar. White pine, in most localities, is so scarce that it is practically prohibitive in price and not to be considered. Moreover, who that had a sense of awesome beauty would ever cut the "Ching-Gwak," monarch of the forest, to build a mere artificial shelter from the storms! Northern cedar has too much of a taper and is "twisty." Western cedar is ideal, for a large cabin especially, but is pretty expensive for the ordinary cabin builder. Norway pine makes a most beautiful cabin, for it is straight and true and tapers little in a reasonable length of log. The coloring of it when oiled is a delight to the eye.

For all-around purposes, balsam and spruce are most practical. Of these two, balsam is the easier to work with. Spruce is inclined to twist somewhat, but is excellent for ridge and purlins owing to its greater strength. Black swamp-spruce is a most beautiful log for cabin-work. If you are near a tamarack swamp where the trees are straight and true and are fair-sized, these can be used, but it is a harder wood and requires more labor. It classes with cedar, however, in defying time. Hemlock is another one of the harder pine trees. Chestnut, birch, oak and other "hard woods" are more difficult to work upon—not only for the fact that they take labor, but they are seldom straight and true enough to utilize as they are. They have to be hewn—or squared up into timbers—before they are practicable. Hundreds of pioneer cabins, however, have been built of them.

Mixing Your Logs

A question often put to me is, "Can I utilize different kinds of logs in the same building?"

You can. Also you may—if you are not too esthetic. The effect of a wall of different sorts of logs even though they may be matched in size is not quite so pleasing to the eye—but far rather different sorts of logs than ill-matched sizes of the same variety. The "shacker's" log cabin is usually formed of alternating telegraph poles and toothpicks and in appearance reminds one forcibly of what Sherman said about war.

In actual experience, I have utilized occasional spruce logs in the walls of a balsam cabin without the difference being observable. In a balsam cabin the ridge or, in fact, all roof logs should be spruce or Norway, for they are stiffer than balsam. Sill logs—which are larger timbers— might better be Norway, spruce or tamarack, but you may do as you like about your rafters in selecting spruce or balsam or any other straight pole. The main point to observe in this selection is that they are evenly matched in size. If you are designating to an old woodsman the straight timber of slight taper, tell him that you want so many "sticks" of designated diameters and lengths.

Type of stockade building with real logs.

where it belongs. In that way a weak, sagging roof can be improved without altering the look of the interior. Often in such an alteration you can add insulation to the roof, but be very careful to keep the insulated space vermin-proof and properly vented. A new roof on top of an old roof will usually create a thicker appearance and thus alter the original lines of the cabin. If the improvement adds structural integrity, then I'd do it, even if it compromises classic lines.

It's unfortunate that Aldrich writes so little about what he calls stockade buildings, with vertical logs. The one he worked on near Trailsyde is a gem. I discuss that cabin, Squantum, in my commentary on chapter 18. Similar to stockade construction is the post-and-sill method, used extensively during the fur trade and often associated with French Canada. I discuss it in my commentary on chapter 19. Both stockade and post-and-sill offer some advantages for log builders with small crews but ample time.

For now, however, let me say that the stockade style is practical because the logs are relatively short and easy to handle. You can buy logs that were cut for pulp. Such logs, delivered by pulp truck, are affordable and fast, compared to hauling full-length logs from a forest area. The major drawback with pulp logs is that your selection of species may be limited. As an alternative, you can recycle logs from old barns or deteriorated cabins. Of course, you have to watch secondhand logs for rot, insects, and nails, but the weathering creates a rustic look for new construction. The effect of the stockade styles is not that of a traditional log cabin, however. Perhaps stockade lends itself best to log exteriors when the interior walls are insulated and paneled for cold climates. An interior of vertical logs can be quite attractve, though log walls of any sort present some problems for interior decoration.

Old porches designed to be open and breezy caught the weather and deteriorated. Tongue-and-grooved flooring dries slowly, allowing more time for mold to begin and rot to follow. Those old porches were probably intended to be torn down and rebuilt every so often. If, however, you rebuild more substantially, you can turn a flimsy porch into a solid addition.

In general, you can skip the porch detailing Aldrich shows for the wooden areas below the screen openings. Intricate patterns of pole or milled frames are in keeping with the Aldrich era, but they are not especially practical. The lower portions of a wall should shed water, not hold it in a network of wood pieces so as to increase deterioration. A smooth, relatively clean lower area is better, and your siding should cover the exposed support logs. Aldrich favored projecting support logs because they have a rustic look, but the exposed ends spread rot. It is true that the original is more interesting to look at, and if you're willing to put up with the yearly attention and repeated repair, then by all means retain the original form as exactly as you can. In many cases, however, I prefer to alter some flaws in order to help preserve an interesting log structure.

With care you can make a modernized porch blend in with the rest of the cabin. I echo some of Aldrich's detail by using batten strips on the siding and board frames around the window openings. Staining can make a big difference, too. A thoughtfully modernized porch needn't stand out like a piece of polished granite in a rough-rock wall.

Aldrich ends this chapter with a discussion of porches. Along Lake Superior's north shore, however, his porches tended to be unused most of the time because the chilly climate discourages people from sitting in the shade of a roof, especially in the evening. The screened porches that Aldrich advocates are more appropriate to locales where summer nights are hot. Nowadays, when people tend to use their cabins more months of the year than in Aldrich's era, an enclosed porch is clearly more practical.

Select Your Special Logs.

After your logs are laid on the ground, make your selection of a fine big log—preferably spruce—for your ridge. Proportionately smaller logs for your purlins. (The sub-ridges that carry across parallel to the ridge between it and the outside wall.) These must be long enough to carry across your room without splicing. If it is not possible to secure them long enough to carry clear across the building and take the projection of the roof, the splicing may be done over a cross wall where it will have the proper support. Next, your rafters should be selected: your finest and best smaller timbers evenly matched—proportioned approximately one-half the diameter of your wall logs. Never use dimension lumber (two-by-fours or two-by-sixes) for roof supports. Remember you are building a log cabin, not a shack. If, for some reason, you must make use of sawed timber, these may be utilized as joists beneath the first floor where they will be out of sight in the finished building. All exposed constructional timber in a log building should be round.

Checking.

The matter of the checking of logs is one about which I am constantly questioned. Despite all that can be done, logs when drying out will open up here and there into seams which to the soul that desires perfection are most disconcerting. Because some of my cabins do not show these checks in the walls, I have been called into consultation by some captains of the lumber industry to know how I prevented it. The admission has to be made that I don't prevent it. I am reasonably sure that nobody can prevent it entirely. But one can prevent its showing in the building and this is what has given me greater credit than is due.

On account of the usual custom of wanting a thing right away, most cabins are built out of logs that are fresh-cut and not seasoned. If one is willing to take the time—possibly select logs this spring for next year's building—they can be cut, scored down opposite sides (which means rip off the bark full length of the log for a strip two inches wide), separated so as not to touch each other upon the skid, and left to dry out for a period of from six months to a year. Then the checking will appear along the line of the scoring, and in placing the logs in the cabin, these checkings, being on opposite sides of the log, can be laid up and down and thus hidden from view. This is merely a trick of the trade.

Stockade Building.

You note, in all these suggestions, I take it for granted that you are planning to lay the logs of your cabin horizontally. If, however, you have only small second growth timber in your neighborhood, you may be forced to choose the stockade type of log building. There are also very satisfactory examples of large logs so placed, notably one in an architect's cabin at Pals' Cove. There are great possibilities in this stockade construction, and he is artist enough to have developed it. The result is a most unique and highly artistic woodland home. Moreover, the shrinkage of his logs, which is often used as an argument against stockade building, seems to have caused him no trouble at all in the calking.

Type of stockade building with "poles."

Length and Size of Logs.

Now reverting to the cabin of horizontally placed logs, their number and size depends, as you might surmise (having gray matter beneath the spot that is gradually growing bald), upon the dimensions of your building. Not that this is invariably true, however—as we shall discover anon.

But even if you are selecting your logs while the plan is only in your head—or, worse luck, in a picture which your wife has culled from the illustration of a story of the Great Out-Of-Doors—you must have some notion of your cabin's dimensions. Also—what sort of help are you counting on in the construction of your building? Unless you are going to have several more in your crew than the average woods-neighborhood affords, you will not want to tackle very long logs even if such are procurable. Twenty to twenty-four feet will give you a one-room cabin (or living room) of sixteen by twenty. For the smaller cabin, logs that will average eight inch diameter are a good size to use. These logs will run about six inch top and ten to twelve inch butt.

The regular way of ordering from a woodsman would be to give him the number of logs you need, the length, and the diameter of the top. Thus, logs for a three or four room cabin should be ordered as eight inch tops to give your unit better scale for the larger building. These, if they run from twenty to thirty feet long, will have butts of twelve or fourteen inches, provided they are carefully selected. Western cedar, which is used for telephone line poles, averages about one inch taper in ten feet. Other timber has a greater taper.

Splicing.

In the discussion of ridge and purlins, I referred to splicing. This is not ideal but, if done correctly, a spliced log may be quite as satisfactory in a building as one that is full length. The main "Don't" to observe in splicing is, "Don't splice it diagonally." It cannot be done thus satisfactorily for either beauty or strength. If you must splice, let it be a "half and half splice." That is, cut each of your logs half through twelve to eighteen inches back from the end and split this half off. Then spike these cutbacks together firmly to make a full, round log, A good splice will hardly be observable unless your building is under microscopic inspection.

Thus far we have been considering logs that are to be peeled. Of course, you are building with peeled logs. For the first year the rusticity of the logs with the bark on may be very attractive, though a romantic young bride and groom who tried this charming effect were driven out of their rustic home the first week by insomnia brought about by the incessant noise of the borers beneath the bark. Even in the daytime, a borer or two sounds as if you had left your engine running, but at night a single one of these log-eaters will make you believe you are living in a sawmill. Then, of course, the rotting of the log begins beneath the bark—after which, the bark falls off. The argument that you have seen old log cabins with the bark still on the logs is beside the point. I am not asserting that all of the bark falls off. Unfortunately, it does not. It comes off in scabs—leaving your new cabin looking moth-eaten. In a cabin whose years justify this effect, it may add to the picturesque. Its age excuses its appearance. It may have a most attractive, rambling, well-preserved look. Personally, I admire these old cabins, when they have good lines, but my suggestion is that if this is the sort you want, buy one ready-made a hundred years old and don't try to build it.

However—there is an important exception to this observation about peeled logs. Cedar bark seems to hang pretty tight and make most artistic porch pillars and railings. Moreover, the flavor of cedar does not seem to appeal so much to the rapacious borer, so one is not likely to have his music in the night time.

Why And When To Peel.

There is a general rule for spruce and balsam logs in the matter of peeling. Winter-cut logs are the best. They should be stacked on skids to keep them off the ground and then in the Spring the peeling is done when the sap left in them begins to warm up and admits of the the bark slipping off easily. In summer-cut logs the bark is tight, and even spruce and balsam will have to be draw-shaved. (Norway and white pine have to be draw-shaved anyhow, so it matters less when they are cut.) Logs cut when the sap is running are the most likely to mildew after they are peeled.

However, one may utilize logs cut any time of year if one follows this direction: Peel the logs. That is, take the bark off. Lay up your logs until they at least partially dry out. Then, to eliminate the discoloring which may have occurred and to prevent future discoloring, go over them with a draw-shave—being careful to cut down under the sap wood. As you know, when you stop to think about it, the sap comes up nearest the new wood-layer forming and this is what discolors your logs. Cedar logs form an exception to the general rule of discoloring. My personal experience with cedar is that it does not discolor through sap. Another point about logs that are merely peeled and not draw-shaved: Stain cannot be successfully applied to them. A light film of sap is left after the peeling which prevents stain from taking effect. Draw-shave into the actual wood, however, and your logs may later be stained if you wish. Even if you merely oil the logs of your main cabin, you may wish the effect of stained pillars on your porch.

A porch which has many uses.

Porches.

There can be cited only one argument against a porch on a log cabin, namely, that the average pioneer type hadn't any. I have heard that argument several times and I have found that two words will refute it, "Too bad!" At least, if it is not adequate refutation, it serves the same purpose—it silences the arguer. Probably the pioneer mother had no time to take advantage of a porch in the daytime, and as for utilizing it at night as we do in our age, it simply wasn't done in pioneer etiquette. The pioneer, even the modern variety, is strongly averse to any possibility of fresh air leaking into his sleeping quarters. In fact, he is almost as fearful of this mischance as many a closed-car addict who goes out for the air with his windows tight shut.

The Tourist Camp at Minnehaha Falls has a roomy porch.

In your general order for logs, include fine specimens of cedar for porch pillars, for your woodsman can probably get some at less cost to you than if you went after them yourself in the general market. Anyhow, even if he makes a few cents off of each log, he probably will make as good use of his profits as the lumber companies would.

As this chapter is devoted to logs, I am not going to take up fireplace material here though that should be as native as your timber. And undoubtedly the one idea you had when you decided to build a cabin was a fireplace with a porch around it far away from civilization. It's a comforting picture to hold in the midst of honks and shrieks and grindings and roarings.

It is as good a nucleus for a Dream Home as any I know.

Logs For Your Porch Pillars.

Nobody can tell you what sort of a porch you want until you have told him what you want it for. Every variety may be adapted and worked out in logs and, however much of an iconoclast you are, you want the thing to conform in some measure to the design of your cabin. If all you want is a platform hooded by an extension of roof to keep the water from dribbling down your neck when you poke your head outside the door to see when it's going to clear up—look about you for some oddly shaped, crooked formation on your trees, some naturally curly or permanently-waved limbs, and utilize them for brackets, bark and all.

CHAPTER SIX

MATERIAL OTHER THAN LOGS TO BE USED IN THE CABIN

Before going any further it is a good scheme to pause in the day's occupation and decide precisely—a word which is defined "with precision, exactitude and in detail"—just what sort of a cabin you are going to have?

So far we know that you have selected a site and that your cabin will be constructed of logs and is to be of a certain type and size. Also it should have been determined by this time whether or no you are limited in time or in money or in distance from the log and lumber market. All these matters eventually affect your building. Now get to work upon design and plan.

Of course, in a book of generalizations upon cabins, every possible variation of the theme cannot be given.

In this chapter can be taken up only those materials which are sure to be needed in your building, aside from logs—and the finishing touches of oiling and staining which will have due discussion later on.

Stone or Concrete?

Just to get a running start, let us begin hunting for rocks. First off, the underpinning necessitates a certain amount of sand, gravel and such rock or stone as you will need, dependent upon whether you are going to use wall or piers or a combination of both. Under "Construction" this will be taken up in greater detail.

Next the fireplace. Not the construction of it or the design of it. Merely the material you are going to need. But in this I am assuming that you are going to have a fireplace of stone if it is in any way possible

Aldrich developed a flair for fireplaces. A fireplace, however, doesn't necessarily represent a wise investment of time, labor, or cash. A fireplace delivers atmosphere and charm, but it can be counterproductive if your space is limited or if you use your cabin in the winter. In my opinion, Aldrich failed to give adequate consideration to heating his cabins because he stayed at Trailsyde primarily during warm weather.

A fireplace will heat a cabin if you have the time to let the entire mass of rock become warm enough to act as a radiator, though a not very efficient one. In cold weather, with frigid temperatures and winds pulling heat from the rock, a fireplace can take a long, long time to become warm. Even at its best, a fireplace draws enormous quantities of warm air from your cabin. Many a vacationer has gone to bed after enjoying a blazing fire and awakened in the morning to a nippy atmosphere made all the more rousing by the multitudes of mosquitoes that found the open flue a convenient route inside, after, of course, every hint of heat had been drawn out of the cabin through the flue. I've been in so many cold rooms with roaring fireplaces that I would prefer to step outdoors and die of exposure rather than endure the torture of roasting on one side while freezing on the other.

Glass fireplace doors may cure fireplace faults, but they look awful on some fireplaces. Fireplaces with rough stone or unusual dimensions or shapes are hard to fit with doors, if not impossible. Adapting doors to difficult openings is apt to be neither quick nor cheap. Doors are not what I want for cold weather.

To me a fireplace insert of cast iron or soapstone is better than a fireplace with doors, because an insert combines the functions of fireplace and stove. With its doors open a good insert does not detract from the charm of a fireplace, and with the doors closed it provides the advantage of a stove for heating. All of this takes up no more floor space than the existing fireplace and hearth. Proper inserts tend to be costly, and they can require special fitting, but they are worth it for efficient wood heating.

Of course, you may decide not to burn your fireplace in winter, which is a practical decision. In that case you can turn to a wood stove or an oil, propane, or electric furnace. In some rural areas you should avoid a heating system that relies on electricity. The storms that knock out the electricity often come in the coldest weather. And a heating system that functions without electricity requires less maintenance of moving parts.

Today you can easily find a wood stove with an insulated stainless-steel chimney kit. Buy an all-fuel chimney made to withstand the rigors of wood burning. A metal chimney will need regular cleaning, just like a masonry stack. Part of your yearly maintenance should include looking for discolored wood near your chimney or stove. Exposed to intense heat over long periods, wood becomes dry and combustible. Areas showing discoloration should be shielded or replaced.

Although I'm less than enthusiastic about stone fireplaces, I appreciate stone chimneys on log cabins. The combination of stone chimney and log wall is visually pleasing, and a solidly built chimney will provide years of secure use. Aldrich wisely preferred round flues, but round flues can be difficult to find. The block chimney with a rectangular liner is common today. But unless faced with stone or brick a block chimney looks out of place when set against log walls. Also, block is porous and prone to damage from extremes in heat and cold, as results from intermittent use during occasional visits throughout the year.

to procure it. Time enough to discuss other fireplace materials when you are sure that you cannot have rock—rough face rock with corners and irregular lines. If you like a "cobble stone" fireplace and if that is all your location yields, use "cobble stones"—but first give them a dose of the spalling hammer. There's a surprise in store for you. You may think that the smooth gray old boulder which was rolled onto your place by some friendly glacier a thousand centuries ago is uninteresting, lifeless, colorless. Split it. Make a rough face upon it. See what a beauty of hue there is inside. That old codger of a stone is like a drab sort of character you may have overlooked all your life. Something happens to break up the uninteresting surface and lo! you have made the discovery of a beauty that gives you a thrill. But—to get back to the fireplace.

Have it colorful. Whatever kind of stones you have at hand, choose among them for a variegated effect in the whole.

It doesn't take a master mason!

There are mighty few places in this best-of-all possible countries where one cannot satisfy his craving for a colorful fireplace. And don't be afraid of rocks with moss and lichens on them if they are sound. In some cases, we have actually chosen the rocks for the beauty of the moss colorings. Often the owner has aided and abetted the growth by wetting it from time to time with a sponge kept for that purpose. About five minutes a week devoted thus to the shrine of Beauty repays you—if you like that sort of thing. It gives a little more the impression of a woodland grotto—that's all.

However you achieve your effect, the face of a log cabin fireplace should be rough. Nothing else harmonizes. Select your material with this in mind.

I must confess that for the fireplaces I build I purchase the best dome damper on the market and also enough firebrick to line the opening—or fire pot. This is not a necessary expenditure, but it is certainly worth the cost. Your warmed open chimney is going to lure every chilly mosquito and fly in the neighborhood the minute your fire is out—which is only one reason for a damper whose main benison is shuting off the cold or damp down-drafts in the room in stormy weather. As for the firebrick—if you had ever seen the results of your hard labor spall away under the chafing of intense heat, or one of your innocent bystanders hit in the eye by a bit of exploding native rock—you would understand why I prefer the unpioneer-like but "safety-first" firebrick for lining. I'll grant you that the brick looks "sissy" before the first fire is built—but after the smoke puts a velvet coating on the stuff you can't tell what it was originally.

Now, having caught your rocks, you will need sand and cement to complete the job. Don't forget that there is a large section of your fireplace that is going to be below ground and that solid footings are necessary. Naturally the amount of material you will need varies with the size and design of your fireplace. It might be well to glance over the chapter on fireplace construction and find out a bit about "weights and measures" if you do not already know them.

The arch of your opening will probably require a steel bar. The forged iron lugs into which your swinging crane is to fit—for, of course, you wish a smoky hanging kettle—might better be purchased along with the rest of the fireplace material, as these must, of course, be inset during the early part of the construction.

Good masonry calls for experience. The work is too important to risk the trial and error of do-it-yourself learning. Make very sure that your mason understands exactly what you want. If you want natural, unsplit rock, he must know that in advance. Sometimes a customer imagines a chimney built of odd-shaped, natural cobbles, only to find a rising monument of dressed stone instead. But it's too late to make changes once the chimney is begun. Be wary of mixing materials or styles in a chimney or fireplace. A cobble rim on a dressed-stone fireplace, for example, will probably not look as good as a rim in matching dressed stone.

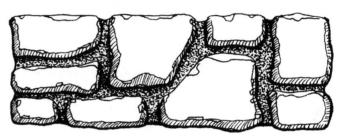

In the choice of lumber for doors and window frames, Aldrich was limited. In those days rural mills could produce only rough or dimension lumber. Today's builder has a superb selection of materials, so Aldrich's comments are only of historical interest now. With extensive rebuilding, as in enclosing an open porch, it makes practical and aesthetic sense to incorporate modern window units to eliminate drafts. With a quaint little bedroom or sunroom, however, you might take pains to keep the room intact. Avoiding factory-made doors and window frames is a problem. Hand-built frames and doors are difficult to replace with contemporary units. Modern windows and doors in a building not styled for them can look horrible. Because doors and windows are highly visible, proceed cautiously in modernizing. If you can't substitute compatible new units with similar styles, you can seek custom millwork or professional rejuvenation of old window sash, although custom millwork is extremely expensive.

If you turn to a professional restoration expert for help in planning alterations, the time and expense must be carefully considered. It can be almost a full-time occupation for a cabin owner or a consultant to keep abreast of the progress of local workmen while also ensuring that materials from distant suppliers arrives on time. Remember that restoration often encounters unforeseen problems and delays that can turn a simple refurbishment into a major structural repair.

It's surprising that Aldrich praises rustic cedar shingles and shakes, because most of his cabin roofs are not sufficiently steep. Wood shingles on a low-pitched roof will leak or rot more quickly than on a steep roof. Aldrich's illustration of a "Finn style" hewn log cabin has a roof of the proper pitch for wood shingles, although a roof with four hips is more difficult than a roof with gables. Furthermore, an important consideration today is insurance. Exposed to external fire or windblown sparks, a shake roof will ignite fairly easily. Some insurance carriers refuse to insure a home that does not have a mineral-surfaced roof, especially in rural areas where wildfire is a hazard and fire protection is limited.

With regard to insurance, keep in mind that many cabins were built at a time of rudimentary building and electrical codes. Substandard wiring is not uncommon. Certain wood stoves and heaters are no longer approved. Using unapproved appliances can negate all or part of your insurance coverage if the fault can be traced to your negligence. An insurance audit can help you uncover problems that could lead to damage or loss of your cabin.

Even if you have full insurance coverage, keep trees at a distance. A tree-embraced cabin is charming, but in a dry season those trees are piles of tinder around your cabin. Excessive growth, long grass, debris, and firewood piles should be kept away from the cabin. Develop a complete plan for dealing with fire, including fire extinguishers and, where possible, a high-volume fire pump and hose for outside protection.

As buildings age, becoming drier and more flammable, regular inspection is vital, especially for fireplaces and chimneys. Chimney flues can develop fissures, and the inner steel shells of some fireplaces can rust through, allowing hot gases to reach combustible materials and woodwork that is tinder-dry after years of slow cooking. More than a few solid old cabins have been destroyed because the seemingly solid rock fireplace allowed flame to ignite a ridge beam or surrounding boards.

The exterior must have good lines.

Lumber.

The lumber you will utilize throughout your cabin will depend pretty much upon what your local market affords. Again a case of the stamp-window spinster: "What kinds have you?" Unless, of course, you can make a grand gesture without even a glance at your last month's bank balance and order what you want from the place that has it—be it the Siberian pea tree.

If your local market is merely a portable sawmill, rough lumber will be all that you can get there, and the lumber you wish dressed will have to be planed by hand unless you can have it shipped in from elsewhere. "Elsewhere" is a big town. Everything for an ideal cabin is to be had there—and every one with whom I have ever had conversation about cabins wished to have an "ideal cabin." Which is as it should be. Ideals, however, differ. One fellow's ideal cabin I discovered when I came to design it, cost fifty thousand dollars to build. Another—to whom I gave one or two hints and a rough sketch—built one for himself which cost him more time, blood and sweat and cussing than money. I don't know which of the two is getting the more fun out of his investment. Both are darn good sports. But one of them was short-suited on time and physical strength and the other on money. In writing this book, I am slanting rather toward the latter—possibly from a fellow feeling. So—to go back to the matter of lumber: How much rough stuff do you want in your cabin—and for what are you going to want it?

In building a small cabin oneself, if one has plenty of time and likes to use tools, it is far more interesting to make all but the glazed items on the job. Of course, your glass will have to be shipped in anyhow, and the hazard is less if it is already made up into windows and French doors—if you are going to pioneer with a foreign accent. And if you decide to order your frames along with the windows and glazed doors, let me suggest that you have them sent to you in a knock-down condition to be assembled on the job, as this will save you considerable in freight.

Otherwise, make all your own frames for the sheer fun of it. Try to disguise your strut as your friends tell you that they never would have believed you could do it!

All frames should be of plank or two-inch lumber because this thickness not only makes firmer frames but—as you will see as you proceed with your construction—it will help materially in stiffening the walls of your building as well as yielding better support for hardware.

While inspecting your fireplace and chimney, check if your masonry is seeping moisture onto your logs. Perhaps the mortar has cracks that allow water to drain into the chimney, or perhaps the chimney is acting like a wick to draw ground moisture. If so, you can install drain tiles to lead water away. In repairing the mortar, you might apply several coats of a sealer such as Val Oil cut fifty-percent with turpentine, followed by one or two coats at full strength. A rain cap over the flue helps keep the chimney dry. If left unattended, rot from a wet chimney can destroy a wall. And dampness and rot are an invitation to carpenter ants. Action when problems begin can prevent major repairs later.

A couple of Aldrich's projects seem to have vanished. The Wa-wa-tay Post, built for the DNR apparently near Ely, with its hand-built furniture has slipped into the fog banks of time.

Wa-wa-tay Post, Minnesota.

Above all things, make your doors on the job. Don't "pick them up." If anything in the world looks like—but I have referred to Sherman's phrase often enough in these pages. Anyhow, a "stock" door which can be "picked up" at a mill does not harmonize—to put it as mildly as I am able—with a log cabin. Keep it for the next tar paper shack you wish to construct.

If you desire absolutely the most beautiful as well as the most harmoniously picturesque door that can be made, demand from your country sawmill the "second run" of the logs—or next to the slab lumber. This will have much of the bark left on it. (If you can manage a White pine or Norway or certain grades of spruce with rich, rough bark, you are luckiest of all!) Not only for doors is this a delight, but anything else can be made of it which you wish to render artistic and unusual. I have utilized it in every possible way. Barge boards are very effective made of it, and cupboard doors, and various pieces of furniture.

Let me state also that it has the amazing peculiarity of being cheaper than the other grades of lumber. Prepare to be snubbed—if not to have your sanity doubted—when you ask for it at any country mill. It is the stepchild of the outfit.

Flooring.

Now—after this burst of enthusiasm over our discovery—let us hit the floor.

Of course, it is possible to have a single floor of matched lumber, but it is advisable to use a double flooring with a heavy felt or other paper between for insulation and tightness. In this case, your under-flooring might be the rough lumber available at the local or portable mill, but, owing to the fact that this is very often uneven in thickness, making the finished floor difficult to lay, it is really much better to count on using dressed shiplap or other matched lumber even for the under-floor.

As to the sort of thing you will have in your finished floor, it depends on your taste and your pocketbook whether it shall be matched pine or fir boards or a regular city hardwood flooring.

Roofing.

We now leap to a consideration of the roof.

Again—rough lumber may be utilized as roof boarding, but it is advisable here, as in the under-floor, to use shiplap or matched boarding. First of all, any unevenness shows in ridges in your finished roofing material. Then—despite all you can do—shrinkage causes the boards to separate, and the prepared roofing is gradually loosened by the wind pressure from beneath through these cracks. If you don't believe me, try it out.

"Oo-ee . . . oo—ow—ee!" screams the wind about the corners of your cabin. "Flap—flap—flap—flap" replies your roof. And you wonder why anybody ever thought that homes in the lumber woods were restful.

Now as to the sort of finished roof you are going to have; shingles, shakes, prepared roofing—or what will you?

Again—all depends upon your design. If you are having a more or less sophisticated home in the woods as much like a town house as it is possible to make it and still be able to refer to it with an affectedly deprecatory gesture as "my shack," you will undoubtedly have shingles. These, properly laid, make a very tight, substantial good-looking roof, but in the ordinary size they seem out of scale.

The real pioneer topped his cabin with shakes. Even today these make by far the most artistic roofing for a log building. If you have the time, shakes twenty-four to thirty-six inches long can be hand-made with precisely the same implement that our ancestors used—the froe. In Kentucky and the Carolinas "shakes" are still handsplit with the froe out of oak, pine or cedar and used to roof the mountaineer's cabin.

There is upon the market a hundred per cent vertical-grain cedar shingle with a drag-face—to give it the effect of the old hand-split shake—one inch thick at the butt and tapered. This is the nearest approach to the old-fashioned shake that is manufactured. In price these are not inexpensive, running about twenty-five dollars a thousand—approximately four times the cost of common shingles per surface covered. If you are deciding upon shakes, however, it is wise to include in your material order a two-ply prepared roofing to sandwich in between the shakes and the roof boarding. Without this layer, you cannot be sure that your roof will be absolutely tight. This roofing is not necessary if you decide on common shingles, but it is always an additional insulation, of course. Shingles are about three times the price of the rolled roofing, and cost more to ship in and more to lay. For a more expensive cabin, asbestos shingles, which have the quality of being fireproof, may be sufficiently artistic to satisfy most tastes if judgment is used in selecting the best in quality and in color. There are many brands of separate shingles made of slate-coated prepared roofing. This same material is also to be had in prepared roofing in rolls, and for a small or inexpensive cabin the best of these is the preferable roof. Further discussion of roofings is found in the following section.

If you are in a slate country, you can certainly secure a highly individualized effect by the use of this atop your logs. Nor do these general suggestions I have made by any means cover all the possibilities of roofing. Try any effect you wish, but make sure that you have a practical, watertight roof. Also one that will not burst into flame the first time a spark touches it. Remember that fire in a forest country is far more of a hazard than in town.

Many ask me about the Swiss chalet roof. I am not going into the construction of this because it is impossible for any but a highly specialized workman to construct it—and the cost of it for an ordinary woods cabin is prohibitive. But—the effect of the chalet roof can be obtained by utilizing poles and rock on top of shakes.

Calking and Chinking.

When you have your logs corralled, you still need a finishing touch in material for walls. Oakum is the best for insulating—and if you are not content with beautifully fitted logs but wish—as many do—a white line between them to set them off—there is a wood fiber plaster on the market which is effective. This is the only material, in my experience, that will "stay put." Ordinary plaster and the mud, utilized somewhat picturesquely, I will admit, by our forebears, will not "stand the gaff." It dries, cracks, and falls out.

The amount of oakum you can fill in depends naturally upon how well your logs are fitted. In a sloppy job of fitting you will need a lot, and your cabin will have to be recalked every year for the greater part of its life. If you are "cupping" your logs, a strip laid along the under log as a bed for the upper one is sufficient. There are other chink filling devices, of course, besides oakum, but—aside from its somewhat picturesque history in shipbuilding and the fascinating tarry smell of it—it not only makes your cabin snug and tight, but it is a preventative of bugs and vermin. A similar office, by the way, is performed for you by the tar paper insulation between your under-floor and the finished one. Especially if you let the ends of your tar paper come up well between the flooring and the walls to keep out any undesirables that might try to effect an entrance in this informal way.

Hardware.

In the matter of hardware as in the matter of mill work, much depends upon what your own neighborhood yields in the way of possibilities. Where is the nearest forge? If there is a spreading chestnut tree in your vicinity, give the village blacksmith a chance. It has been my experience that the average member of this far-famed guild knows a lot more than he is ever called upon to demonstrate. Given an opportunity, I am willing to wager that he will amaze you with his eagerness to undertake your simple designs and with his skill in executing them. Otherwise—your hardware dealer in town can supply you with everything you need—even to the hand-wrought effect.

Speaking of nails, don't forget that twelve-inch spikes are seldom to be had in the woods—so get your order in early. Personally I specify an oval head, three-eighths inch by twelve-inch chisel pointed wire spike. For the rest, the nearest village will supply your needs in nails required, but remember the old adage, "Git a plenty while you're gittin' "—for shortage of nails has held up many a job and caused almost as much of a catastrophe as the lack of a horseshoe nail in one of Mr. McGuffey's readers. If you buy your nails by the keg, you will pay about the same price for a lot of them that you will pay for half the quantity in any other bulk. So—use your judgment.

A Word To The Unwise.

Take note that in this discussion of materials needed, I am assuming that you are at least superintending your own building—even if you are not actually a horny-handed son of toil yourself. If you are going in for electric lighting and plumbing of every sort, there is only one thing to do: Commission an architect who knows not only his own specialized form of city work, but knows logs and has studied, first hand, the conditions in your "neck of the woods." Wiring and piping through logs is a very different operation from the wiring and piping in a town house. For—if you have any sense of humor—much less sense of harmony and beauty—you are not going to let the pipes and wires of civilization disgrace the native simplicity of your logs by crisscrossing their sturdy lines.

What shall you order first? Gosh, man, I don't know. Windows probably. Hasn't the good wife already finished the curtains for them so that you know precisely what the sizes are?

Tools.

But there is one thing certain: You are going to need tools. All that are in the handy kit at home and then some. Aside from ordinary carpenter tools, you will need a cross-cut saw, a double-bitted ax—which is sometimes informally called a "two-bit" ax—two or three cant-hooks for handling the logs, a broad-ax or a regular adze, which can be used in average work instead of a broad-ax, one or two heavy gouges, the curved bit adze, or howel, and at least one shipwright's "slick"—which is a big heavy chisel three feet long, with a blade three inches wide. Many of these tools were used in the old pioneer days and were then hand-made. For example, the howel for cupping the logs is seldom on the market, but it can be formed from the ordinary adze by the village blacksmith. The number of these tools needed depends on the size of your crew at work.

For your mortar mixing, you will need a hoe and a mortar box—which, of course, you will make on the job—being careful that it has slanted ends like a scow. Six foot length gives you a chance to work your material over and over. Ten to twelve inches is a convenient depth. One of the most important instruments of torture is the grindstone. If a speedometer had been affixed to ours in the job I finished while beginning this book, it would have registered about fifty thousand miles by actual count of the eighteen men on the crew. Of course, it goes without saying that you will have on hand a level, a trisquare, and a six-pound stone hammer, which will "double in brass"—or does duty both in log work and masonry.

BOOK TWO
CONSTRUCTION

CHAPTER SEVEN

UNDERPINNINGS—FOUNDATION WALL—OR BASEMENT?

"All set—Let's go!"

(Thus the shout from the throats of the fifteen hundred "gobs" who, during eventful 1917 and '18, were building cantonments under my supervision. No other phrase gives the same effect of sleeves rolled up and hands spit upon, ready for work.)

We have the cabin staked out, our materials assembled near the site, the workmen on the job. "All set—let's go!" It's easy—if you know how.

First of all, inside the lines of the building clear away all your big trees, utilizing what you can—and of the small live things, transplanting as many as you think will grow well. Don't let your crew begin with ruthless upheaval. Strike the keynote at once or they will probably have the place looking as if an earthquake had brought up your cabin from the depths of destruction instead of giving it the appearance of having grown up like a mushroom amid its surroundings of untouched beauty. Don't think that because a man lives in the woods all of his life he is a lover of wood things—the very familiarity with them often makes him contemptuous. The abomination of desolation about the first cabin I built—despite all I could do—still makes me sick in retrospect. In "Seven Glens"—a construction of thirty-two by forty feet over all—even the trees which touched the sides of the building when it was completed were unharmed—and the moss still clung to the nearby rocks.

After we had staked out the building, we dug away from the ground within the lines all that might be a fire hazard or carry smoldering running fire, and piled up the rocks about the location marked for the fireplace. Then the peeled logs were brought up from the lake, where they rode at ease, and dried.

Everything rests upon the foundation, yet Aldrich touches on the topic with a casual concern. Working along the Lake Superior shore, where almost everything rests upon solid rock, perhaps he became slack in his standards. He probably planned to keep his relatively small cabins plumb by shimming as needed to compensate for the shrinkage of logs or settling of stone supports. By now most of Aldrich's cabins are out of plumb, some by a great degree. Trailsyde is the worst: any attempt to open the south-facing windows leads to a battle royal because the window frames are so distorted from settling. The south wall has sunk at both corners, while the massive fireplace has remained on its proper footing, creating an eave line with noticeable undulations.

Aldrich's tendency to use one or two rocks set upon a flat rock footing worked only for the short term. Uneven settling was inevitable with these rocks of insubstantial footing. A first step in assessing your cabin is to examine your foundation closely, especially if part of your cabin rests close to the earth. Damaged supports or sections with woodwork near the ground should get remedial attention before you invest in other improvements. The fact that the entire building rests upon the foundation seems to escape the notice of many cabin owners, who envision redecorating the interior as a major improvement. Having decided on new rugs for the bedroom floor, they spend not a moment's worry on the integrity of the floor itself. Most of us prefer to tackle superficial, easy problems than to engage in fundamental and often difficult structural repairs, even when putting off the needed work allows further deterioration of the building. Virtually all cabin owners are quick to agree, but when they take a look at the old cabin at the start of another season, they usually suffer a sudden attack of lost will. After all, the cabin has lasted a long time without major work, so why go through all that bother now, just before summer when the cabin should be enjoyed, not worked on?

I have heard nearly every manner of excuse, rationalization, and justification for not rectifying structural faults. I always remind cabin owners that their increased demands on the structure have added to the problem, especially if they're thinking of eventually retiring to the cabin or adding a spare room for the grandchildren. A cabin built for light seasonal use cannot become a year-round dwelling without extensive reconstruction. Indeed, sometimes much of the previous work on a cabin must first be undone before setting things right. I can't tell you what a look I get for suggesting that.

Think of it this way. The original cabin was seasonal and simple. The walls were of plain log, and the early additions were uninsulated shells that breathed with the seasons. Then, for example, the family decides to spend a Thanksgiving at the cabin. They discover that the floor is chilly and that their cozy little summer place is beastly cold during a long early-winter night. So improvements are made. But each bit of upgrading encourages more use and more piecemeal improvements.

They tack fiberglass insulation onto the underside of the floor in the crawlspace to conquer the chilly floor. Inside, they add false ceilings with insulation, perhaps without a proper vapor barrier. In effect, they are putting the bark back on a tree and letting it lie in the damp woods to decay. Insulation and vapor barriers will often trap moisture that previously escaped through the cabin's pores. Deterioration begins, often unnoticed, and dark molds flourish, discoloring and destroying the

Underpinning.

Ready now for the underpinning or supports for your sill logs.

For underpinning the average cabin, upon the average soil, rock is used. Make sure that your rocks are honest-to-goodness boulders dug into solid ground. Select them for their more or less flat surfaces, so they will firmly hold your logs—or another flattish stone, if necessary, to build one on another for height. If all the rocks in your vicinity are rounded by the glacial roll, here is an opportunity to use that six-pound stone hammer, which is part of your equipment. Spall off a flat place to bed the other rock or the sill logs.

Rock rests upon underground concrete pier.

If your ground is yielding, you will have to build concrete piers for your boulders to rest upon. The depth of these piers below the forest floor depends on how soon you reach solid ground. In extreme cases, I have gone through clay soil as deep as six feet, putting a sand and gravel cushion one foot thick in the bottom of the hole, and building upon this a concrete pier up to grade level. Then—for the looks of the thing—I rest boulders upon this to support the sill logs, as boulders are more in keeping with a woods environment than is concrete.

In using any variety of underpinning, the main thing is, of course, to make sure it is solidly bedded and to level up well. In utilizing boulders, this is no easy task and you will realize as never before that there are no two things in Nature the same size.

Method of bolting sill log to foundation.

wood. After a few years the cabin acquires a faint odor of mildew, and mice move into the insulated spaces that had formerly been open. Mice are especially fond of false ceilings.

Meanwhile, other improvements are taking their long-term toll. A home in the city was designed to have a bathtub full of water in the bathroom, but the summer cabin was often not planned that way, so the added tub and other appliances and furniture have added some sway to the lightly built floor. And what about the electrical wiring added when the cabin was decades old?

You can, of course, simply resign yourself to making occasional repairs of trouble spots and let it go at that. Stop-gap measures are better than none, although they may hide serious damage under layers of bandages. But it's better to correct basic problems than to work around them. Truly big faults require an overall strategy to make the repairs in careful stages as you can afford them, while leaving the cabin useful in the meantime. Complex problems or conditions that require speedy work, such as replacing the roof, are often too much for the do-it-yourself owner and a few friends. Capable professional workers, however, can be difficult to find and expensive to hire.

It's not easy to tell in advance whether a carpenter pays close attention to detail or skims along with the breezes. One of the best craftsmen I've known was an older man with a blunt manner and sour expression. His tact with potential customers was woefully lacking, and many people refused to hire him because he was "too darned cranky." But his work was as painstakingly perfect as his manner was rough. He was never short of work because his quality was high. Customers tended to leave him alone to do his work, which was, after all, what he loved and what the customer was paying for.

In contrast to him, a carpenter with a pleasant personality may have rave reviews from past clients, but you can't always rely on a good repu-tation, because many cabin owners don't know the difference between sound work and slipshod. In general, your cabin is in safer hands when a carpenter expresses reservations about certain phases of a project and asks questions about what you hope to achieve. You'll be able to tell quite a lot by how methodical and detailed the carpenter is in assessing the work. Beware the hammer-wielding dolt who says, "Nothing to it.

We'll have it fixed in no time and be out of here." Be prepared to pay a satisfactory wage. And remember that money and labor invested in improving a cabin is largely wasted if the effort fails to correct underlying faults. Sometimes you must go right down to the foundation before starting back up.

As Aldrich states, a cabin foundation of piers will allow the building to breathe well, but it will be cold-floored in winter, whereas a full foundation helps keep out cold winds and unwanted guests, such as the crawl-space skunk. Getting a full foundation under a building that lacks one, however, is a formidable undertaking beyond most do-it-yourselfers. Even if you know how to proceed, you'll probably have to ask someone about the local building codes. You'll have to locate and examine all the water, sewage, gas, fuel-oil, phone, and electric lines in the ground. A full foundation will restrict access in the future, so update the utility services before you add a solid foundation.

To place a solid foundation under an existing building, you must first put foundation footings in position. Footings are the wide concrete base that supports the narrower foundation wall. Your footings should be below the frost line, so your cabin will not shift from surface heaving with each freeze and thaw. To get below the frost line requires much digging, but because your cabin is already there, you usually can't use mechanical equipment. You will have to do the footings piecemeal or bring in house-moving equipment to support the cabin during excavation. An eave wall is generally more load bearing than a gable wall, and the corners and the center of a wall, especially an eave wall, are heavily loaded: those areas must be well supported. Piecemeal footings should be tied together with steel extending from one piece to the next. The bottom log of each wall must be anchored to the new foundation wall with bolts or heavy spikes set into mortar.

On a log cabin a foundation of native stone looks best, although a stone foundation requires a lot more and effort than a block wall. While waiting a few days for a footing to cure up, gather and lay out the materials for a rock wall. I lay out entire sections of wall dry before mortaring it, to make sure I'll have enough stone. On paper it sounds easy enough. In practice it entails a great deal of back-taxing labor. The cabin is always in the way. You're constantly stooping and bending into grotesque positions while maneuvering heavy stones into place. And, of

Concrete Mixtures.

This is probably as good a time as any to talk about mixtures of concrete, as you are assuredly going to use more or less of it, whatever sort of cabin you build.

In mixing it for piers, basement walls, fireplace footings and so forth, a fool-proof mixture is one part of Portland cement, two of sand, three of gravel (about two-inch size). However, a sufficiently rich mixture, if properly done, is one part cement, three parts sand and four of rock or gravel. Mortar for laying up stone work is one part cement, three of sand. In all mixtures, hydrated lime should be ten per cent of the bulk of the cement.

Remember that in your aggregate any old sand or gravel will not do. Sand must be coarse and sharp, and both must be clean—which means free from organic matter—no loam or clay. Unfortunately, in the case of sand, the human eye cannot determine its cleanliness. The only way to be sure is to have it analyzed. Either do it yourself by writing the nearest Portland cement mill to send you the color-metric test—or send direct to this mill a generous sample of sand (about five pounds in weight) and ask them to test it for you. They will do it gladly. As to gravel, of course, if you have creek-bed gravel or lake-shore gravel, you can be pretty sure of its being well washed.

A little hint in building your piers which will save you time and concrete: Make the box forms taper from the bottom up. Say twenty to twenty-four inches square on the bottom and one foot square at the top—or at grade level. This furnishes sufficient surface to rest your boulder upon and at the same time gives you firm footings at bottom. Another trick it turns is that it saves labor by making the forms easy to slip off when the concrete is set. Thus you may utilize the same form for another pier. Two or three well-made forms ought to be sufficient for your building.

Increasing Your Aggregate.

Now—here is a notation which finds place along with the suggestions for mixing concrete: In pouring the walls of the basement or in the base for your fireplace, small boulders may be dropped in the mixture up to fifteen per cent of the bulk of the whole—provided said boulders do not come in contact with each other. In other words, use your common sense about spacing them and don't bunch them. Of course, the boulders must be clean—like the rest of the aggregate.

Foundation Wall.

Suppose you are ambitious enough to attempt a foundation wall or even a basement. There are good reasons for a wall, although a cabin set upon boulders allows the air to circulate freely beneath it and keeps it dry throughout the year. But a foundation there must be if you plan to live in your cabin during cold weather. Even in hunting season, the floors will seem pretty chilly o' mornings if you are a tenderfoot. Moreover, a wall will effectually shut out night prowlers either of the striped-back variety or other sorts that depend on racketing around for their chief dissipation. "Knock-turnal" visitors such as rabbits, stray cats, squirrels, porkies and their ilk can sound like an army of elephants oft in the stilly night. Of course, stone or cement is not needed to keep out these—as a picturesque arrangement of poles or split logs placed closely enough together will do the work—and still permit the air to range at will beneath your floors. Accordingly, insulation is your only vital reason for having a foundation wall.

This will be constructed either of stone, concrete, or concrete with stone facing. Personally I would hide the concrete, if I were doing it. You will note, by the way, that in giving materials, I have not mentioned brick. To my mind, any manufactured product of this kind is incongruous with logs, though brick is beautiful for construction either alone or in combination with less primitive building material. You see, a cabin is presumably a native product—constructed, preferably, of materials locally indigenous. I have seen brick fireplaces in log cabins, but to me they always seem to sound a false note. However—if you happen not to feel that way about it, try out your brick by all means. For the same reason, I have suggested concealing the concrete—though in its rough form it is not inharmonious. And it has the virtue of being made on the job.

Your first step in foundation is to excavate a ditch along your lines down to a firm footing below surface soil—through humus or black dirt —called the "forest floor." Of course, if you are on rock—that settles it. In this event, the next step is not necessary, for you can begin to construct your wall at once upon native rock.

Having reached sand or gravel or any type of solid ground, pour into your trench the "footings" of properly mixed concrete at least once and a half the width of the wall you are going to build—depending upon the firmness of the ground—and about six to ten inches thick. The idea of course, you have the added challenge of working with stones and logs, uneven materials that complicate your efforts to keep the foundation level and true.

As for leveling, you should bring the floors to level before doing the foundation rim. Allow the building to adjust gradually over several days to correct the alignment after having spent years out of plumb. While leveling, your interior posts or piers will need attention, too. Those are the hard to get at ones tucked way under the floor. You need stable new footings and a rot-proof support. Crawling beneath the cabin with wet concrete and other materials is no fun, but it is necessary for a complete job.

It would be ideal if your entire cabin could be moved out of the way while a new foundation was constructed, but with a fireplace, especially on an interior wall, raising a cabin is both expensive and beyond the abilities of the typical weekend carpenter and friends. Invariably, cost and time lead to other practical compromises as well. A crawl space, for example, should include a poured concrete floor several inches thick in order to block vermin and ensure a sealed dry area below the cabin. A crawl-space floor, unlike a basement floor, can undulate with the lay of the land. My father used to navigate his rolling crawl-space floor on a car creeper, scooting along to fix the plumbing.

It is a major undertaking to insert a full foundation rim under a cabin. But if the old building has sufficient charm or value, then all improvements should contribute to the structure. With a secure foundation that keeps your cabin on the level, that part of your past known as "the summer place" will serve future generations. And you'll feel great satisfaction in having completed a full foundation on your own. Each rock will have some meaning, as will the way you framed in the vent openings and placed the access opening, even if others give scarcely a glance at your achievement. Indeed, if they assume the foundation has always been there, then you've done a competent job. Others may slip rigid foam insulation between their floor supports to cure a cold floor without the labor of a foundation, or they may install wooden barriers because they're easier to construct. But your masonry foundation will outlast its substitutes. You won't have to make annual trips under your cabin to correct areas where rodents or ants have attacked the foam board. You won't be stuck with an old wooden foundation skirt rotting into uselessness.

Of course, you need extensive technical know-how to build a foundation. If you've never done masonry work, spend some time helping someone who has. Then try a minor project at your cabin or home before tackling your foundation.

If a foundation is simply out of the question, then take care in adding insulation under the floors. In the crawl space under a cabin, Styrofoam is easier to install than fiberglass and easier to protect from mice. Because old subflooring is usually uneven and full of gaps and cracks, take extra pains to ensure a good seal between the Styrofoam and the subfloor. Caulk the gaps and cracks that extend outdoors and allow cold air to infiltrate between the insulation sheet and floor. Put a bead of sealant around the edge of each Styrofoam sheet before snugging it into place with cap nails. Each floor stringer log should be tightly caulked as well.

If vermin chew through your foam, cut the chewed section out and caulk in and seal a new piece. Rodents often follow the scent trails left by previous generations. Wetting gnawed areas with bleach or a disinfectant solution weakens the scent trail. For continued chewing, put in a stronger barrier such as hardware cloth. Watch for signs of ants, especially at the exposed areas closest to the ground, but remember that ants can infest areas anywhere, from sill log to ridge beam.

footings is, as you know, to spread the weight of the building, and in any but the most uncertain of soils eight inches is deep enough. On this footing build a board form to your general grade—that is, to the point at which you have decided your first log is to lie. (Preferably a foot above the highest point of your grade.) Into this form pour the properly mixed concrete—and "let 'er set." This is the base for your floor joists.

Of course, at advantageous points you will want to put two or three openings in your wall on opposite sides of the building for circulation of air. These openings may be merely frames with wire screening—but preferably frames with quarter or half inch mesh wire screen and a hinged batten shutter which may be closed in cold weather.

Now if you have the same feeling that I have about this matter of keeping in tune with the woods, you will probably wish to face up the exposed part of your concrete wall with a rough stone facing. In this case, you will build your outside board form only to grade—letting the back form of the wall carry up to the level of your floor joists. Then build a shell of rock for the outside facing from grade up to this same level, filling in with concrete as you go, between this and the boarding.

It is advisable to bury in the top of the stone wall iron bolts at intervals of possibly six to eight feet, dependent upon basement windows, corners and length of wall. These bolts must project above top of the wall a distance equal to the diameter of your first log. Thus are the first logs of the building bolted to the foundation.

Basement.

The first suggestion I should make, if you are set upon having either a full-depth basement or a partial one, is to find somebody who knows how to build it and have him make you a proposition. There are problems simple enough to an experienced hand which a novice in the work—or one who knows more about the theory than the practice—is going to have some difficulty in solving.

Not that you are going to believe this when you read the general direction that all you have to do is to make your excavation as deep as you need and build your walls precisely as you build the foundation wall—only more of it. But be not deceived, friend, be not deceived. By the time you have had your walls slide into your lopsided excavation two or three times, because the forms were not properly wired and braced, you will realize that you would have saved time, money, and the expenses of a divorce suit—brought on by profane babblings—if you had hired in the first place somebody who had had experience.

But—be that as it may or what you will—your wall is up. At this time, or after the roof is on, a basement floor of cement may be laid. To prepare for this, first tamp down the dirt until it is as hard packed as a tennis court. (The end of a log makes a good tamper.) Then spread upon this hard surface about a three-inch grout—or layer—of concrete, finished on top with a three-quarter-inch richer mixture, say one to one, of the sand and cement floated on before the grout is thoroughly set.

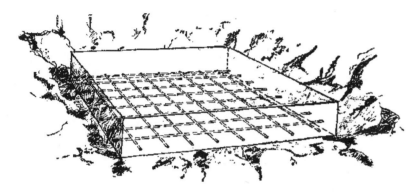

Fireplace footings showing steel rod "mesh."

Fireplace Footings.

Now, right along with the rest of your firm foundations, you are putting in the footings for your fireplace—so, of course, you know precisely what sort of a fireplace it is going to be. If, at this point, you have not decided upon all the "trimmin's," however, you must know at least the measurements of your fireplace plus your hearth and whether or no it is going to be a skimpy affair or a massive one, weighty in masonry.

Fireplace Proportions.

Although this matter is to be taken up in the chapter upon fireplace construction, you must know somewhat about proportions right now. If you have not an intuitive feeling for proportion, you are out of luck. Ask your wife—women usually have a good eye for balance—and then get a consensus of opinion of your friends. By that time, if you are not a candidate for the sanitarium, you will probably do precisely as you had decided to do in the first place.

Too small a fireplace for the size of the room in which it stands gives the whole the air of a playhouse—too large leaves you breathless with a sense of being overpowered. But if you must err, overdo your mass rather than underdo it.

I don't want to give any rigid mathematical suggestion on proportions —for these are born and not made—but in actual experience I have discovered that each one of the fireplaces I have built approximates in width one-third the longest dimension of the room in which it is placed. This is massive—but will not give the effect of being overwhelming.

The projection of your fireplace footing is the same as the projection for the footings of your wall—or about six to eight inches beyond the measurement of the fireplace plus hearth. This is a solid slab of concrete in which are placed steel rods ten inches on center both ways (crisscross) as a precaution against settling. These rods, wired together at intersections, make a steel mesh which is well worth the slight extra expense in preventing any possible cracking in the masonry above.

One varies the thickness of the slab, of course, with the weight of the fireplace and the yield of the ground. Somewhere from eight to twelve inches is safe, and the steel rods should be placed a few inches up from the bottom of it.

After this slab is set, build board forms properly wired and braced to avoid spreading and fill up to the point which marks the bottom edge of the floor joists with concrete and small boulders as described for walls. Block in a board form the width of the hearth. Then fill in the fireplace proper to the top of the floor joists. This board, set back, leaves the concrete below the level of the finished floor to receive hearthstones later. Further details of fireplace building are to be found in a chapter devoted to this construction.

At this point you are—or you ought to be—ready for log work.

CHAPTER EIGHT

HOW TO LAY UP YOUR LOGS

Upon Boulder Underpinning

Having leveled up your boulder underpinning, lay your sill logs—which are drawn from your longest and strongest suit, so to speak, across them lengthwise of the building. For artistic effect, let them project beyond the building line and have the ends ax-cut.

All logs, by the way, are to have ax-cut ends where they project. If your building is narrow, you can manage with two sill logs. If it is wide, the floor joists would best be supported by another laid through the center. These logs may be cut somewhat if necessary to make them bed well onto the stone. And remember that, from first to last, your level is always on the job. Yes—undoubtedly you have seen cabins built without the use of a level. So have I—seen them at a glance, in fact.

With the sill logs placed, the end logs are laid the width of the building, notched into the sill logs and spiked into place. Thus the frame is formed to start your walls. See that your corners are right angles. In other words, square up your building.

Types of Fitting.

At this point the question has already arisen, what sort of notches are you going to have and what sort of fitting for your logs? The answer to this question depends on the time, money and labor you are willing to put into your building.

(A). When a man is pressed for all three, or is building for himself, he is likely to decide upon the rough "saddle and notch" for the corners and lay the logs together without fitting—or "trimming out." The

The style of the times preferred cabins, casual structures, close to the ground. Only houses had high foundations and steps leading up to them. So Aldrich often shows a log wall supported by a mere one-rock elevation above soil level. In one way or another, today's cabin owner must repeatedly fight deterioration caused by that condition.

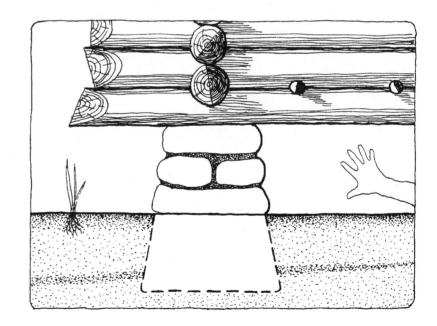

Aldrich's description of setting up and then laying log walls is rather rudimentary. You can find other books that are more detailed. Then, to really learn how to handle logs, take a course from someone who's good at it, as carpentry skills require hands-on experience.

Aldrich was not himself the best log fitter, and his truly good work seems to have depended on skilled log workers. One of the men who worked on the cabins in Hovland was a skilled log fitter, J. Myhr, but Aldrich apparently did not learn much from this man, who later supervised the construction of some fine cabins with large logs finely scribed and matched. As a result, Aldrich fails to discuss log scribing fully. Perhaps a professional architect was above taking lessons from a local worker with no credentials other than talent and experience.

"Saddle and notch" corner construction.

spaces are afterward calked with oakum. This saves time and labor and therefore money, but is not the type that one chooses either if he wishes the most beautiful log work possible or if he is going to utilize his cabin for cold weather.

(B). In what may be called "hewn and fitted" log work, greater care is used with the same "saddle and notch" corner by dropping it so close that the logs have to be hewn for fitting—that is, the contacting surfaces must be flat to lie together neatly. In this method, calking may be done after the building is completed.

(C). A third type of fitting uses the same "saddle and notch" corner with "cupped" logs. In this, the lower log is left as it is and the upper log is cupped or hollow-cut its full length to fit down closely over the log below. To secure the best effect in workmanship, use a pair of pencil dividers to scribe one log to the other. Thus, all irregularities are noted as you follow Roosevelt's motto of hewing to the line and letting the chips fall where they may. This sounds so easy that a few fool-proof directions might be in order: Roll the log into its place and make a saddle in the cross log just deep enough to bring the upper log sufficiently close to the lower to be able to scribe it with your dividers. Then roll the log back and hollow it out to the line by use of ax or curved blade adze or heavy gouges. Then cut the notch deep enough to receive the log, which is then rolled into place. This process may have to be gone through several times before the log lies in perfect fitted position.

It is quite likely that you will fall short of perfection—but when you are satisfied that it is time to quit, roll your log back once more and string a heavy layer of oakum upon the lower log. Then comes the final roll of the cupped log back into the position it will occupy for a century or more if left alone. Spike it down tight.

(D). The fourth and finest type of fitting for corners and lengths is to cup one log to the other lengthwise and cope one log over the other at the corners. In this corner coping the lower log is not cut at all. The upper log is hollowed out to fit, gripping the lower closely where it crosses it in the same fashion as your hand grips the stair rail. The oakum is strung along the lower log and laid in at the corners in all types, of course.

When this fitting is properly done, no oakum will show anywhere and the logs look as if they grew together. No calking ever need be done afterward. This type it is advisable to use in the finest work, as it gives a beauty to the completed building that is possible with no other type. You are well repaid for time, labor and expense.

Spiking.

A word about spiking your logs may properly be introduced here: Each log is to be spiked at the ends and every few feet in length with the twelve-inch spikes as specified heretofore. These are amply sufficient for the ordinary sized logs in a none too intricate cabin design.

However, as sometimes happens, if these are not to be found within reasonable shipping distance—three-eighths-inch rods can undoubtedly be had at the nearest blacksmith shop. These rods can be cut any length desired, pointed and used as a substitute for the spikes. Occasionally, one may wish to go through two or even three logs with one spike, and in this case these rods will have to be used, as the twelve-inch spike is the longest obtainable on the market.

Even so, I have used the large spike successfully with logs that were twelve inches in diameter by boring a hole half the distance through the upper log and then using a driving pin to send the spike home well into the log below. Here again your six-pound stone hammer comes into play. Make sure that you have a goodly length of spike penetration into your lower log, for upon your spiking depends much of the stability of your building. Logs will wriggle a bit whenever they have a chance— even the best of them.

Floor Joists.

In a boulder and sill-log basic construction—after the frame is made—floor joists of smaller logs should be notched into the sill logs. It is more artistic, of course, to have these joist ends, ax cut, project beyond the outside lines of the wall, four to six inches. Lay your first joist next to the wall log and space them not over three feet on center. It is advisable to hew them on top before they go into the building because in this way you will find it easier to produce a level condition to receive your flooring. If you are having a stone or cement wall foundation—either with or without a basement—you will probably prefer to use two by ten or two by twelve plank joists if they are obtainable near by. These joists rest upon your stone or concrete wall. Great care must be taken in leveling up your joists both throughout their length and with each other.

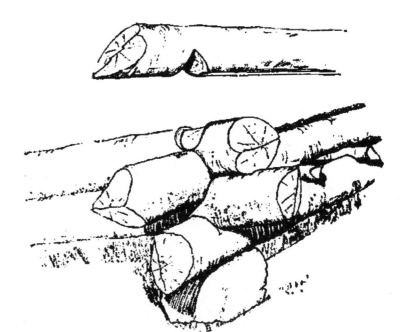

Round "saddle and notch" corner.

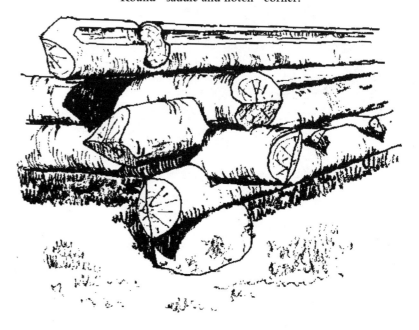

Coping and cupping.

Cross wall built into outside wall.

Walls.

Having chosen your type of log work, keep to the same style of fitting throughout your building. Carry up the outer walls of your building and the partitions or cross walls at the same time, for these too must be properly notched and fitted and tied into the main walls.

Keep in mind that one of the most picturesque features of the log cabin is the random projection of the ax-cut ends of the logs from a few inches even to two or three feet beyond the building line.

If the occupant of the log cabin under construction needed no more air than does the present-day trapper, a cabin would be easy enough to build. A trapper frequently does away with what he considers such artificialities of civilization as windows and constructs a small opening for a door through which he can thrust his doubled-up body and lets it go at that, fastening it up tight for the night. One wonders after inspection of the living conditions of some of them what the average length of life of a trapper may be. It is somewhat disconcerting to find them old and gray and hardy beyond civilized ken. We are forced to the conclusion that they absorb so much air during the day that their lungs are allowed to rest at night along with their other organs.

However, the average woodsman has a window in his abiding place. The old way—and the modern way where timber is cheap—is to build the wall to the line that marks the top of the opening—be it door or window—and then saw it down as far as one wants it with a cross-cut saw, both sides of the opening. In other words, build your cabin like a box and cut your windows and doors out afterward.

However, as short logs cost less and are more easily manageable than long ones, the better way is to run your wall logs a few inches beyond the line of the opening and then when the top of the opening is reached, place a straight-edge or board on both sides of it and, with a cross-cut saw, cut the logs down to receive the plank frame which is ready to be put into place.

First of all see that the frame is set plumb. Then spike it to all ends of logs—two spikes in each log-end if you wish to make sure the log will not twist away from it. In setting these spikes, be sure to place them so that they will be covered eventually by the "stop" or the inner finish frame.

To avoid the effect of being tossed lightly into place—windows and doors should have at least a few lines in common. Although it is not necessary for the tops of windows and doors to be in line, it gives a good effect, especially in a small cabin. The top line of the glass in the windows should be above the eye line of the average person.

Frames.

The frames should be made of two-inch dressed plank—of a width, obviously, that approximates the average diameter of your logs for top and sides. The sill should be of plank two inches wider, projecting over the log wall to form a drip and pitched down one inch. Usually two to three logs above your frame will bring you up to a proper height of wall. There should be at least one log between the frame and the plate log.

As a final reminder which bears iteration and reiteration, make sure that your logs are strongly spiked together in your walls and the corners firmly fitted. The wall of a log-lodge in a would-be summer resort none too far away from our North Shore cabin swings to and fro in a heavy wind. Unless you are building a wren house, avoid this contretemps. And once again—see that your walls are carried up plumb and true and the frames of doors and windows set square. Don't attempt to save your level and your trisquare for another job. Wear them out on this.

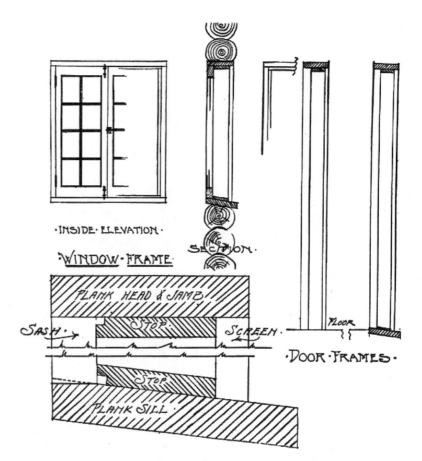

Construction of frames.

Low pitch and wide eaves are picturesque.

CHAPTER NINE

GABLE ENDS, EAVES, RIDGE LOG, PURLINS AND RAFTERS

Now, just as a balanced diet includes not only the staff of life with a slice of meat between—but also a salad and a sweet—so your cabin's stability and the straight, true lines which have been stressed so much need beauty and harmony with a dash of the picturesque to set them off to full advantage.

In a vacation home of this sort, be careful of an over formality even in your architecture. This does not mean sloppy workmanship. Far from it. Slip-shoddiness is a vice—not an informality. It means that one may take a few liberties in exaggeration of line for quaint effect. That sort of thing. Your doors may be somewhat lower than those of your town house. But don't have them so low that you bump your head every time you pass through. Casement windows may be wide and low, and roof lines may be long and inclined to a flatness which is seldom allowable elsewhere.

Don't let any remark of mine to the effect that cabin-eaves, like donkeys' ears, are more picturesque if worn rather wide, lead you into the vice of overdoing the matter. Proportion plays a part here as everywhere. A small child with a ten-gallon cowboy hat upon its head may look cute as the dickens to fond papa and mama who will take his picture from every angle for admiring friends to behold—but that sort of grotesquerie is to be cannily avoided in your cabin. Study the pictures of your favorite log buildings—be they chalets, pioneer cabins or logging camps—and then work out your roof projection.

Take plenty of time to consider just what effect you wish to produce, and then take plenty of time studying the best way of producing that

The photo preceding this chapter shows Aldrich's work at its best and worst. For this cabin, wherever it was located, Aldrich wisely gave the roof more pitch than he gave to his other cabins. The detailing, however, amounts to a rustic version of Victorian gingerbread. The area below the screened openings of the porch is busy with water-catching projections and protruding logs. The exposed purlins and rafter ends are also vulnerable to water-induced decay. Rot damages decoration soaked by rain or splash, as well as shaded and moist areas. Logs projecting from walls fare somewhat better, because they are protected by the eaves or gables.

Several modifications are advisable. The projecting porch timbers should be cut flush with the floor edge, and the whole porch system should be covered in a skirt of, for example, cedar plywood to shield the exposed wood, including all the timber ends. These changes will alter the appearance of the porch noticeably, but batten strips can provide a semblance of the original look. The purlin and rafter ends should be trimmed back to cut away the rot. Cedar fascia board could cover the raw ends.

If the rotten timber ends have spread decay into the adjacent roof boards, extensive roof repairs may be necessary. The fascia-edged roof won't look as rustic as the original, but it will be less prone to decay. As an alternative to cutting off the exposed purlin and rafter ends, the rotten portions could be cut off and replaced with new pieces of log jointed or pinned, but such cosmetic repairs would weaken the roof edge. I'd choose to eliminate the areas destined to rapid deterioration.

You can preserve a cabin if you are faithful about maintenance. Cover exposed pieces of pulin with copper (not aluminum) sheeting. Caulk areas that catch water. Weathered wood should be scraped, wire-brushed, or sanded before you add new coats of sealer. On porous weathered surfaces, cut your varnish with turpentine by thirty percent, so the mixture will penetrate deeply into the wood. You may need four coats of thinned varnish before the wood is properly sealed and you're ready for uncut varnish. Concentrate on the trouble spots, rather than revarnishing the entire cabin for each coat.

Alternate view—Kitchen Entrance

effect. After all, you are your own doctor. If some sort of a freak cabin pleases you most go to it and blithely face the frank criticisms of your friends or their swiftly averted glances and the pain of silent anguish writ large upon their brows. No less a personage than Abraham Lincoln is reputed to have observed, upon occasion, that, if people like that sort of thing, it is precisely the sort of thing they like. No adequate rejoinder has ever been found to flatten out that remark.

And right here, along with these more or less general and sapient comments, let it go on record that I have indicated the futility of following out to the letter the directions or suggestions of any book upon any subject.

There is, the most devout among us may proclaim, one Book whose directions will provide perfection if one holds to the very letter—but as nobody ever followed these printed directions without variation from spirit or detail thereof, experimental disproof of my assertion is still wanting.

Building the Gable Ends.

When it comes to the construction of gable ends, one must have determined precisely how far he wishes his ridge to project, how wide the eaves are to be and at what angle he wishes his roof to be pitched.

Roof bracketted over kitchen entrance. (Entrance not shown.)

Many old-timers and modern conservative builders will opine, with sad shaking of the head, that one must have a steep roof in a part of the country where the snowfall is likely to be heavy. Yet the low pitch of the Swiss roofs belies this. Low pitch and wide eaves certainly make for the picturesque effect. A pleasing pitch for the roof of a smallish cabin is a rise of about four inches to the running foot—increasing this slightly for larger building.

Anyhow, having decided upon this angle, whatever it is, build the gable ends to the peak where the ridge log is to lie. Then the gable ends are hewn down along the line you have marked for the slopes of your roof until an even surface is obtained upon which the boarding is to rest.

Ridge and Purlins.

Awhile ago I spoke about putting one's best sticks foremost as ridge logs and purlins and rafters for the vain and simple reason that these are going to be constantly under—or over—inspection. The ridge log especially should be a beauty, and the setting of it a ceremony. There are two or three methods of carrying out this ceremony, and the purlins may be built through the gable end in several ways, as the latter proceeds in its construction.

The easiest, and a substantial way, is to hollow into the gable log where you wish to set your purlin and cope the next piece of log in your gable over it. Other methods are squaring and shouldering it in as described further on in a discussion of the setting of rafters into the plate logs.

But the main point is that, as the construction of the gable ends proceeds, purlins must be set into them firmly to carry the roof—hollowed into them with a bed of oakum added to make a tight job. These purlins will be placed low enough so that later on the rafters will set into them a little for firmness' sake. Again—if the ridge log and the purlins are set down two or three inches below the roof boarding line, one avoids the labor of cutting all the rafters into them—as must be done at the plate logs. Make sure that they will extend beyond the lines of the building six or eight inches farther than the boarding of the roof to allow for projecting ax-cut ends.

After the gable end log upon which the ridge is to rest has been hollowed out to receive it by whatever method you elect, the ridge is rolled into place, bedded in oakum. Then a cap forming the peak of the

Varnishes with ultraviolet-ray inhibitors and fungicides are good for older logs where deterioration has begun. Paint sellers or manufacturers can show you compatible products and additives. Some suppliers recommend urethane plastic finishes instead of the old-fashioned marine or spar varnishes. These newer finishes don't always bond well on the older cabins that were originally treated with varnishes of natural oils, however, so I'd varnish a small test area and leave it exposed to the weather for a year before making my decision.

Walk around your newly oiled cabin on a rainy day and examine how well the water beads and rolls off. The areas that are still absorbing water need further varnishing once they have dried out. Check especially dark or black areas. And don't forget to use your ladder.

In this chapter Aldrich describes one of his favorite features, skylights, which he installed in most of his cabins. Modern skylights, fortunately, are similar in size and proportion, so they're easy to replace if necessary. The principal advantage is ventilation, so I favor skylights that can be opened. If there are trees that could hit the roof, use a storm cover when the cabin is unoccupied.

Aldrich's false ceilings enhanced two cozy rustic bedrooms in the Totem Pole Lodge. His sketch shows a symmetrical design, but the actual building is not evenly balanced: the false ceiling on the outside wall is pitched less steeply than the one on the inside wall. Despite the coziness, these false ceilings create hard-to-reach pockets where the false ceiling and the roof merge, ideal for a mouse nest to grow larger year by year.

For his false ceilings Aldrich used dressed shiplap, so they're smooth, clean, and mellow with age. Aldrich had learned to use only milled shiplap for ceilings and roofs from his first cabin, Trailsyde, for which he used rough lumber raw from the mill without curing. As the boards dried, the ceiling formed gaps large enough to admit vermin. As soon as Aldrich plugged one hole with tarred oakum, the little critters would unplug another. Adlrich turned to milled lumber with side joints that gave a good seal.

In this chapter Aldrich includes pictures of some larger log buildings. The first seems to be the interior of the previously shown building with a prominent dressed stone fireplace. The building seems to have served a

public function of some sort. Its location is unknown, apparently not on Lake Superior's north shore.

The next two pictures show Croixsyde, completed around 1926 after four years of effort. With prime logs brought from the West and a skilled crew brought from Finland, Aldrich created a magnificent building that is listed in the National Register of Historic Places. His client, Mr. Sheffield, desired a log building on a lavish scale, with galleries, overhangs, lofts, and a grand stairway. The logs were scribed, matched, and fitted to perfection. All the electrical wiring was hidden inside the logs with the help of a local blacksmith who made long extensions for his drills. He also built curved electrical faceplates and other hand-wrought features, from door latches to chandeliers.

Although Croixsyde is a far cry from Aldrich's ideal of a cozy little log cabin, he merely expanded and glorified the elements he favored for lesser structures. The dining room at Croixsyde is reminiscent of the dining area in Squantum. Similarly, carved posts and rails grace both Croixsyde and Squantum, although Squantum's posts are colored. The false ceilings of the Totem Pole Lodge are echoed in the upper bedrooms of Croixsyde, where each bedroom has the perfect proportions of s snug little log cabin tucked away in the woods. As in smaller cabins, Aldrich gave Croixsyde green woodwork, walnut-brown flors, and similar detailing on the porch. A tour of Croixsyde, which the present owners allowed me, is like taking inventory of Aldrich's whole career in log cabins.

gable—shaped of either one or two pieces of log—is scribed to the ridge and fitted down over it.

An effective gable and porch (unfinished).

Rafters.

Having set the purlins and ridge log, the next to consider are the rafters. These also are your trump sticks for straight, non-tapering lines. Have them gracefully proportioned, too, to the purlins—which, in turn, are somewhat smaller logs than the ridge. Too small rafters will look like toothpicks in a large building—while too large will appear to threaten the life and limb of those who pass beneath them. In a small cabin, four inches at the butt with easy taper is a pleasing size—increasing to a six-inch butt in a large cabin.

Various methods of setting rafters into the plate were indicated a few minutes ago: squaring them in—which is the easier and rougher way of doing it—or, with more time and labor, making a nice shouldered job of it with an appearance of perfect fitting. The easiest of all is to cut a V-notch in the plate log and chamfer off two sides of the rafter to fit this notch. Bed with oakum—as in the case of ridge and purlins—before driving it home to stay.

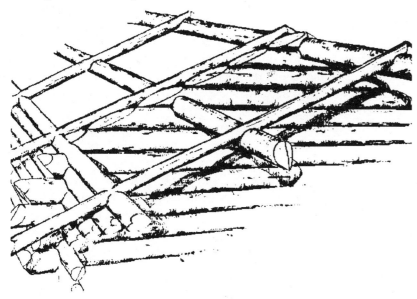

Ridge, purlin and rafters at gable end.

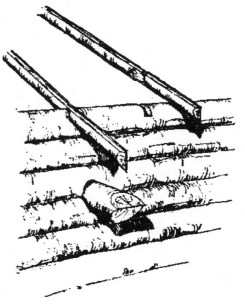

Detail of rafters and plate log.

To square the rafter into place, saw a square cut into the plate log large enough to take the rafter which has been squared at this point of contact to fit it. Then sink the latter into place, flush with the plate log, bedding in oakum for tightness' sake.

"Shouldering it in" is much the same method as squaring it in except that in addition to the squared shaft of the rafter, which fits into the squared channel of the plate log, the rafter is accurately scribed, perfectly fitted and coped to it.

The upper end of the rafter rests upon the ridge and is spiked into stability here and upon each of the purlins, into which it is slightly cut to rest tightly. They should be set not more than three feet on center and flattened or hewn down on the top side to make a true and even surface for the roof boarding. This work may be done with an adze after the rafter is set in place—or on the ground before placing it—using a broad-ax.

Speaking of Roofs.

Dressed and matched lumber, or shiplap, is preferably used for the roof boarding, as we discovered in the chapter discussing materials. This is nailed to the gable ends, rafters, and plate logs. A layer of oakum is strung along plate logs and gables first to make all tight.

Roofing.

The different kinds of roofing have also been pretty thoroughly discussed in the chapter on materials. Here we will merely recapitulate.

The very cheapest roofing which is practical to use for a log cabin is a two-ply prepared roofing which will last from five to seven years. Quite frankly speaking, you will not like the looks of it upon a building you value. And the cost of a better roof which enhances the beauty of your building and will last from fifteen to twenty years is not enough more to warrant your thrift. In short—it is seldom thrift in the end to buy as cheaply as possible.

There are roofings on the market of the better or "slate-kote" variety which are worth the additional cost. If you are careful to buy that on which the slate—or rough surface—is not carried to the edge, you will then have a smooth surface of about two inches for lapping and cementing firmly. This make the tightest job.

There are many composition shingles on the market at about three times the original cost of the composition roll-roofing and two to three times the cost in labor of laying, per amount of surface covered. They make a very pleasing roof and, to the notion of many, might be considered well worth the additional expense—merely for the effect of a shingled roof.

If, however, your decision rests upon a composition roll roofing of any variety, don't fail to roll it out upon your roof boarding and expose it to the sun for at least an hour or two to give it its stretch. Then lay it while it is warm, seeing that it is well cemented at the joints and nailed closely. (Personally I specify every three inches.) The reason for laying it while it is warm is obviously to avoid the crinkling or buckling which takes place when it is laid cold and then proceeds to stretch itself out in the warm sun.

Common shingles are laid in the usual way directly on the shiplap boarding.

One might give the same non-explicit directions about laying shakes—except that in some parts of the country the "usual way" of laying them might not be understood. . . . (Although in any section of the country where logging is—or has been—an industry—they are a not-familiar sight.) Usually made of pine or cedar, they beautify lumber camp buildings to a degree of picturesqueness that invariably attracts the wandering artist in search of material for his pencil or brush.

Shakes, then, are laid as shingles are laid but with an exposure to the weather which falls just short of half their length. In a twenty-four-inch shake, for example, about ten inches to the weather—or in three-foot, the largest size—a sixteen-inch exposure is best both for picturesque effect and for practical reasons.

To gain the appearance of a chalet roof—although let me remind you that it is not the actual Swiss construction—long poles, stayed with rocks at intervals, may be laid upon the roof.

For a "double roof" or especial insulation where the cabin is to be used in the coldest of winter weather—on the boarding as above noted—lay a two-ply composition roofing reaching only to the outer edge of all outside walls. Nail 2x2 wood strips on this roofing at outside edge of the boarding around the entire building, over each rafter, at gable ends, and at outer edge of all wall lines, as furring strips. On these strips, and projecting one inch at the outer edge of roof all around, lay another boarding and proceed with your finish roofing. This gives you a two-inch air space of insulation.

Skylights.

Before we leave playing around on the roof, let's gnaw a bone of contention among cabin builders. To have or not to have—skylights!

Personally, I am going to come out flat-footedly and announce that I am all for them. If you are to dwell among trees, your cabin is going to be gloomy unless you have so many windows that they give your place the privacy of a gold fish. Many a "no-neverer" in the matter of skylights, after seeing the added cheeriness they give, especially on a rainy day, has gone home and desperately cut a hole in his own roof.

Not only in the living-room is the skylight a comfort. Particularly in the room utilized as a kitchen, the light from above is a boon. A "practicable" skylight—as the stage would call it—will emit smoke and odors of cooking to the outer air instead of to the lungs of the cook and the noses of the guests. It may have a curtain over it to shut off the light on too sunny days, and it may be—yea, it must be—screened.

In constructing the skylight, the frame of it should be several inches above the roof level and adequate flashings provided about it to prevent the seepage of rain or melting snows. These may be of tin or galvanized iron, painted to tone in with the roof covering. Sheet lead flashings are more expensive, but they are almost everlasting.

When ordering the sash at the mill, order the skylight window along with the rest. A good conservative sixe is 24x30 and one and three-fourths inches thick. Rather than the lapped panes of the hothouse type, it is best to have three lights of glass the full length of the sash. If you specify in your mill order that these are skylight sash, they will be made in proper detail.

Right here one might suggest that you will need covers for these when you leave your vacation home. Wooden box-like affairs that fit properly and fasten down will be all right.

Ceilings—True and False.

Of course, it is possible to conceal the underside of the roof boarding in any number of ways, but the sensible thing is merely to give it a touch of decoration, and call it a ceiling. A false ceiling is not a mere covering

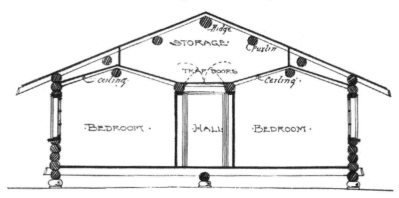

False ceiling.

for the boarding but an entirely new construction, giving the effect to any room in which it is used of being a separate little cabin. In fact, this appearance, along with the purpose of proving storage, is the false ceiling's raison d'être.

Now for construction: build into the main walls of the building at the height desired for the room, the ridge log of the new ceiling and—after the fashion described for laying rafters—place the poles, or false rafters, upon it, tying them into the other two walls of your room at the angle which makes the desired slope of your new ceiling. It may be a much flatter effect if you wish—than the roof. Then lay matched boards upon these in the manner suggested for the roof. The space between this false ceiling and the roof may be reached from the inside by a trap door.

An effect of beams and trusses.

Trusses.

Although it is obviously impossible to go into detail in the discussion of a pretentious cabin, one may say that, where rooms are of considerable size, it may be necessary to put one or more trusses across to prevent the roof sagging. Of course, this enhances the picturesque effect of your interior, for you are going to utilize only beautiful logs for this additional support. Often it is necessary to lay only a couple of logs—in reality the lower cord of a truss—across the room, as a tie from wall to walll. Vertical supports may be run from these to the ridge and purlins, thus securing a truss effect. All this is extremely picturesque as well as being serviceable construction, but these structural problems are not for the novice.

Real trusses may be things of beauty.

End of a galleried living room.

To jump to the other extreme—if you are really going in for the effective in logs, and don't care who pays the piper—there are heaps of things that can be done which will be joys forever. Swiss balconies with hand hewn railings—galleries and lofts, as well as beautiful and complicated truss work which has meaning and use added to sheer beauty. But, in the name of the great god Pan, don't try to secure any of these effects without competent workmen.

Galleries and Lofts.

While we are having a lot of fun, however, imagining that we have at command all the money we wish to foot the bills of an inspired designer and expert superintendent along with experienced workmen under his supervision, we may let our imagination run riot among all sorts of quaint and beautiful effects possible to achieve in the interior of a log building. Without presenting too much of a real obstacle to the novice, one may say that a loft thrown across the end of the living room, even of a smallish cabin, may add marvelously to the beauty of the room if designed with an eye to proportion and constructed by a hand that hath cunning. This nucleus of beauty may be expanded under expert superintendence to broad galleries with suites of rooms opening from it.

Stairs.

Along with these effects of two story—or mezzanine—a means of approach must be furnished. A ladder is the more picturesque and takes up no space, but stairs offer less possibilities of damage suits from rotund guests.

The artistic appearance of your stairway is immeasurably enhanced if the treads are of log material and not boards. To be "shoppy" a bit, I usually specify treads of large logs, saw-split through the diameter—briefly, half logs—rounded off at the ends and projecting beyond the stringers far enough to take the hand hewn balusters which are dowelled to the rail.

A stairway can make—or break—the interior of a log building.

But don't let the beautiful dream of what may be possible in the way of construction, lure your mind away from the grim necessity of what must be actual. A roof, for example, is not so romantic as a Romeo and Juliet balcony—but it is far more to the point to have a successful covering than a picturesque overhang.

Figuratively speaking, it was the leaks in the parental roof which caused Shakespeare's romantic lovers to seek the dry seclusion of the tomb—wasn't it?

Who was it, anyhow, that gave the sapient advice about trusting in God—but keeping your powder dry? Well—substituting the word roof for powder, the same is an excellent adage to follow in cabin building.

Detail of stairs.

Fireplace at "Seven Glens."

CHAPTER TEN

FIREPLACES

There may be more important things in the cabin than the fireplace, but the average cabin builder never discovers them. Anyhow—let's have a corking fireplace wherever else we may have to fall down. If your walls are constructed with rank disregard for proportion and your floors weave up and down, and your windows rattle in the summer breezes so that you have to shout to make yourself heard above their din, and worst of all—in a rain storm you hear a gentle drip, drip, not upon the roof but upon the floor below the roof—be able to make a grand gesture and say as one who over-lords these scant efficiencies—

"But—where in the countryside is there such a fireplace?"

Don't think that a joyous harmony is achieved by a tossing together of rocks helter-skelter, chinked with gobs of mortar. The fireplace must be the most carefully thought out and lovingly constructed part of your Dream House. It is in the fireplace, too, that individual taste finds its greatest opportunity for expression. So, make up your mind that nothing in your cabin is so difficult, so fascinating, so satisfactory in results as a successful fireplace.

. . . Just keep in mind three sina qua nons:

It must be in harmony not only with the architecture of the cabin but also the woodsy environment.

It must be beautiful in its proportions—not only of a general size and shape to suit the room, but also in its related parts.

It must draw well and throw out heat.

As long as you keep to native material the first of these will be difficult to escape. The rocks of your fireplace are going to look as if

For Aldrich a log cabin wasn't complete until it had a hand-built fireplace, huge or tiny. I'm not as enthusiastic about them myself. And I won't elaborate on construction details, because most log-cabin fireplaces, added later, are steel fireplace units with heat-saver ducts. If you, however, want to hand-build a fireplace, consider Aldrich's source, the Rumford fireplace method, devised by Count Rumford around the time of the American Revolution. For lining the firebox, soapstone is preferable to common firebrick.

With rough, natural stones Aldrich created fireplaces both rustic and attractive. He often made his openings taller than the mouths of typical fireplaces, and as a result his fireplaces smoked badly. If you could use stone as effectively as he did while following a better plan, your fireplace would be a lasting asset. It might be worth the effort because metal fireplace liners are made of sheet steel, and they deteriorate. The combination of moisture-retaining masonry and occasional high temperatures ensures corrosion. A hand-built fireplace, which is all masonry except for the heavy damper and dome, won't turn into a pile of rust, and its firebox is safer. If you have a metal fireplace, you should inspect it once a year. As the liner deteriorates, dangerous gases or heat can escape. Your cabin could burn down because of a rusted-out fireplace liner.

At both Trailsyde and Seven Glens, Aldrich put holes in his fireplace floors for cooking beans slowly. These bean holes are inconvenient. Although the fireplace floor is quite hot, it's difficult to get at your bean pot, and debris falls into the hole whenever you lift the cover. The bean

holes would have worked better in the side walls of the fireplace, as in Colonial ovens.

The tiny fireplace in Crow's Nest draws well and is attractive. Several of the smaller stones in the interior are set at whimsy, and a few have initials carved in them. An exterior stone has the words "SOCK GREEN," probably the name of someone who worked on the Crow's Nest. Perched on the edge of a cliff, the Crow's Nest apparently fostered a high degree of personal attachment in those who built it.

The picture of the Crow's Nest fireplace shows rough cedar planks split for the ceiling and roof. The chimney flashing is peeled back and obscures the chimney behind it. The split-plank roof was too rough for roofing, so a layer of boards was put over the planks, and then the roofing was added. The space between planks and boards was sealed with oakum. A plank-roof ceiling is a bad idea because mice and bats will infiltrate.

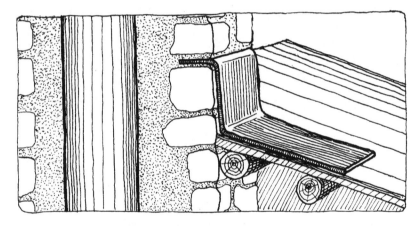

Illustration of Flashing.

they belonged there if they actually do belong here. One of the fireplaces pictured herewith, built of rock within easy hauling distance, is so identical in coloring and carefully massed ruggedness with the cliff visible just beyond it through an open window that it gives the wall of the large living room the effect of having been hewn out of the cliff itself.

All right then—have you the best of your mind with you? If so—let's think this thing out together, for building a "point-to-with-pride" fireplace is no mere child's play.

Much has been said hitherto about the materials and the mixtures and that sort of thing. (Look back and see if I'm not right about it.) Now—

Regardless of whether or no you have a basement, the base of your fireplace must begin where your house begins or lower, and it must be carried up to the level of the first floor as the building goes up. At this point, it is possible to go ahead with your building and fit in the fireplace after your roof is on—or even at some future time—when there is more money, more material, or more leisure. However—and make a note of this—it is not so satisfactory as a fireplace tied in with the cabin as it progresses. There is always the difficulty of making a neat job of it—and if the fireplace is in the midst of your building, there will doubtless be cross walls to be set into it and these are much better placed if the stone work and the log work are progressing together. Moreover, your fireplace can be made a veritable bulwark of strength to your building by proceeding with the masonry as the log partitions ascend—tying your logs right into the rock and mortar structure.

Materials.

As suggested before somewhere, brick seems incongruous with log work. I don't know why. It may be my own feeling rather than a settled fact of Art. Maybe it's because God made the trees and the stones and man made the bricks. But stay—let it be the fundamentalism of the glacial stone fireplace of the present instead of the brimstone fireplace of the future that we discuss in this chapter.

Almost any sort of stone may be utilized. Beware, however, of the softer sandstone. There is nearly always a native supply of rock within hauling distance of any place you are likely to build. Glacial drift boulders—or field stones as they are called by the natives—quarry stone or ledge rock. The latter, of course, has the picturesque rough face without remodeling it, but it is desirable to bring out the inner beauty of the drab, smooth field stones by splitting them with a stone hammer or bull point and a sledge. However, not only is the rough surface obtained for the sake of beauty, but the stone is often chipped off for flat surfaces to bed it securely.

If possible, kidnap a mason—for when one comes to the point of actually telling another how to lay up stonework, one becomes strangely reluctant either of making a fool of himself by explaining in too great detail or of being too unspecific in direction. But in case you have determined to go ahead and do this job yourself, one sadly selects the former of the alternatives.

Friend, do your part by at least studying into the principle of things before you lay a stone or mix a single box of mortar. And if you can casually get hold of a mason, you might ask him in an off-hand manner a few questions about bonding stones. If you happen not to know what bonding is, he may tell you that it indicates the proper placing of a stone so that it will lap the joint of the stones below—and you will be so much ahead, anyhow.

Bring in plenty of rocks from which to choose and have them at hand. Look over your pile and select those that you wish for your first course. Have regard for size, color and the position they are to occupy. If I hadn't seen so many amateur fireplaces, I might not think it necessary to make the suggestion that the larger stones be utilized for the lower part of the face, letting them grow smaller as you progress. Every once in so often—pretty often, if fact, stand aside and admire your work. There is excellent precedent for this in the first chapter of Genesis. Repeat your creed: "I believe in Harmony, Symmetry, Proportion."

Mortar.

Now just to impress it upon your mind at the time you need it most, let me repeat what is elsewhere found in this volume, the proper mixture for stone laying mortar is one portion of cement to three of clean, sharp, coarse sand. These two ingredients, together with ten per cent (of the bulk of cement) of hydrated lime must be mixed well. Hoe it over—dry—until your back breaks. Then add just enough water to make a proper consistency—keeping rather to the error of having it too dry than too wet to use with your trowel. Practice on it until you get the right mixture before you ruin your best stones by having it squeeze out from between them and dribble down their bright and shining faces. You need merely enough water, you know, to crystallize the cement.

Aldrich's round flues in his chimneys make some masons blink in disbelief. Building such a flue is a slow process, and the flue is likely to crack eventually because it's too solid. I've never seen an Aldrich flue crack, however. His solid rubble-filled chimneys are tougher than tough. I've tried to batter a new hole for a thimble into one of his chimneys, and it was like trying to hammer through solid rock.

His chimney caps are sound and attractive, although flue covers, to reduce the rain entering the flue, would make them better. On Trailsyde he had to extend the chimney in order to create a longer flue that would draw better.

The picture below shows the Trailsyde fireplace with Aldrich on the right. Notice the straight line from his chin to the pipe in his guest's hand. That line is the bottom edge of the smoke lip that Aldrich added to tame his smoking fireplace.

After sixty years of soot accumulation, the Trailsyde fireplace looked like a mass of dirty rock. A lot of scrubbing and careful use of an acid wash revealed the natural stone again. Once it's clean, a fireplace that's prone to dirty itself should be give repeated coats of a sealer like Val Oil to prevent the grime from reentering the rock pores.

Laying the Corner Stone.

Now, having placed with a flourish the first trowel of mortar upon a corner of your cement base—to construct which you have read, marked, learned and inwardly digested Chapter Seven of this volume—you call your relatives and friends to witness the laying of the corner stone of your fireplace. Have them ready with the ceremony. I have no suggestion with this except to see to it that both the ceremony and the stone are rather snappy.

Then proceed around your first course with the stones you have selected, and fill in the joints between the stones with the mortar. Bond the stones of your following course each time, and don't go too far with your shell until you begin to fill in back of it with concrete. Two or three stones high might be enough for an amateur to manage before backing it. Make sure, by the way—that your shell wall has set sufficiently to hold before filling. Over night is usually long enough to let it stand. Perhaps it would be well to emphasize here a matter which will be perfectly clear to you from the illustrations: that all fireplaces which I build or design are constructed with the opening up from the floor at least one course of stonework, that is, from one to two feet above floor level. To the mind of those who see this construction, it is more artistic and unusual—but that is not the whole reason for it by any means. The heat comes out direct, is thrown out farther into the room, and the consequent circulation of air gives better ventilation.

Another reason is that it is less back-breaking work to build and tend a fire in them, and if you are making a show of cooking over them, it's a lot easier when the fire-chamber is raised above the floor. If you wish a beanhole in the fireplace, a pit is easily built on the floor of it and covered with a piece of boiler plate a quarter inch thick, cut to fit. It can be built up square of firebrick—or the "drum" method may be used as described later for flues. Frankly speaking, the bean hole does not seem to be an extremely practicable addition to a fireplace. Theoretically, it's great—but after the first few times of making use of this pioneer method of bringing the beans and the bacon to the breakfast table, it has been discarded for some reason in favor of the oven-baked pot. Possibly, it's because we of to-day are too darn lazy to take the trouble to cover the fire as carefully as our ancestors were wont to do.

To Rake or Not to Rake.

Right here determine whether or not you are going to have flush joints throughout your stonework, or joints that are "raked out." Like the nursery-rhyme folk who are not at one in their tastes about "pease porridge"—some liking it hot and some liking it cold—the matter of joints is entirely to your own taste. "Some like 'em flush," but we like 'em raked —for raking them will define the outline of your stones, yielding soft shadows that enhance the beauty of the masonry. Try it and see for yourself what you gain by the use of a spike, scraping out from three-fourths to an inch deep along your joints after the stone has been set several hours.

Firebrick Lining.

The firebrick lining which you are putting in because the stone is likely to spall off in the intense heat of a wood fire, is carried up according to design about the height of your stonework in a mixture of equal portions of sand and cement—not forgetting hydrated lime. The brick may be laid upon edge or flatwise—on edge in a small fireplace, flat for the larger.

The space between this and the shell of stone (after both are "set") is filled in with concrete mixture proportioned as before specified for piers and bases. Upon this, the wall may be continued as before, following your properly made design, the firebrick being laid up plumb at the back for about fifteen inches and then drawn in as it rises to form a throat for the damper. The sides are carried up plumb, splayed three to six inches on each side according to the width of the opening. Thus the back dimension of the floor of the fireplace will be six to twelve inches less than the width of the opening.

Damper.

Somewhere in the foregoing chapters it was suggested that the best dome damper on the market should be brought to the job. It has arrived, crated, and has been moved about from place to place to get it out of the way. Now is the time for its final move. If you would rather not have the brass handle sticking out of the front of your stonework, and giving away your concession to modern comfort, the damper you have selected has the side operating bar which may be successfully concealed from the casual eye. The handle may be even recessed if you wish,

Fireplace at Crow's Nest.

in the stonework. Anyhow—regardless of how you operate it—the damper is set upon the firebrick and a smoke shelf is built at the bottom of it about twelve inches deep and the length of the damper.

The Arch.

Having built the stone facing up to the top of the opening, an arch bar should be put in place. An iron bar, three-fourths by three inches, is necessary in the opening of a large fireplace; but in a smaller size—or ordinary opening—a bar of the dimensions of one-half by two inches will suffice. This may be either a horizontal bar or, preferably, if you wish an arched effect it may be given a camber—or bend—to suit your artistic eye. A slight camber also has its practical advantage. Back of this bar a wooden form is built—set back far enough to constitute a soffit—or under side of the stone arch—of about five inches. This form pitches back to the front edge of the dome damper and must be braced into place.

Now, when I am about to go to work upon any particular section of masonry, I utilize the simple and childlike method of selecting the stones and laying 'em out on the floor about as I plan them to be built into the mass. Having done this with the arch stones, going in for as variegated an effect as my material will allow in the rocks, they are then placed on the iron arch bar bedded in mortar. The stones should be thin enough—front to back—to allow of from one to three inches of rich concrete or cement mortar, mixed one to two, to be placed as a backing between the stones and the wooden form up to the edge of the damper. In this rich mixture of cement mortar are arranged reinforcing rods across the back of the arch and hooked into the sides of the stonework of the fireplace. The first one of these rods is placed within an inch of the back of the arch and so on up through the chimney breast above the shelf at intervals of about six inches on center. Remember that the mortar is to be kept to a reasonably dry mixture, for here is the place where it is sure to be messy if it oozes out.

The Family Catch-all.

Now if you are going to have a so-called mantel shelf whereon may be placed all the pretty little stones gathered by the family—and literally licked into colorfulness—all the bits of moss that dribble black dirt but are glorious atop with tiny fairy gardens, all the shells, fungi, or crooked tree growths which some imaginative member of the family has decided look just like a snake or a shepherd's crook or a man with one eye—or, in brief, any of the fascinating collections of oddments which occur in all the best regulated cabins . . . now is the time to build in the shelf to hold 'em.

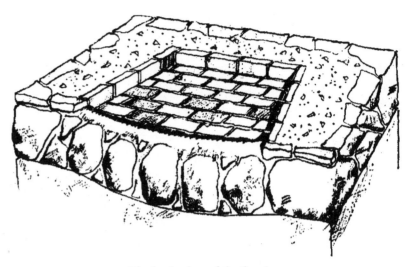

The beginning of the fireplace.

The mantel stone will be flat. It's often difficult to find stones flat enough unless you have the luck we had—of discovering an old quarry. Then we cut on out to suit ourselves. Anyhow, the stones should be ledge or quarry rock—in dimensions about four to six inches thick by twelve inches deep to give a really worthwhile shelf. If you must use more than one stone to produce the length you wish, have a reasonable uniformity in them, for the love o' Heaven, and set the shelf well above the arch opening. In a small fireplace it may be as low as four and a half feet from the floor, but in larger structures five to six feet above the floor line is better. The shelf stones must be set to project into the mass far enough so that as you build up above the shelf these latter stones may rest upon it and help to hold them in place. Until you have built up far enough to hold the shelf in this fashion, it is wise to have a support beneath built up to keep the mantel stones from tipping out and discouraging you to the point of announcing in firm tones and with many emphatic phrases that you will be eternally dad-bummed if you ever try to build anything again by following some blank fool's written directions. And—unnecessary to observe—as you build the shelf and the front of the fireplace, you are going ahead with the whole shell of it so that the walls are all about the same level. If you must have a wooden shelf—a hewn log will work out to the best advantage. This may be anchored into stonework with lag screws or spikes driven into back of log and stonework or mortar built up around them, thus fastening them in.

If you like wide, flush joints in your stonework.

The Smoke Chamber.

Now comes the trick of a good fireplace. At least, one of the tricks. An adequate smoke chamber. Beginning on the level smoke shelf—this combustion chamber is formed equal in capacity to one-fourth of the capacity of the fire chamber. There are several methods of achieving a successful smoke chamber: a wooden form may be built as inside form and concrete poured around it, or it may be built up of the firebrick as used in the lining below. In any event, the sides and back should be built up straight about the width of the smoke shelf—or twelve inches—and the front should pitch back following along the angle—or pitch—of the backing up of the arch to the dome damper. From this point the back carries straight up, and the two sides pitch in at about a forty-five degree angle, the front being continued upward at the same pitch as that at which it started. Thus—all tend to converge toward the opening—or beginning point—of the flue. This will vary in diameter from fourteen to twenty-four inches dependent upon the size of the fireplace. (This phrase would sound well in a Greek chorus, wouldn't it?)

If you have utilized the wooden form method of building the smoke chamber, this form, which was made collapsible, is now taken out through the opening made for the flue entrance, after the concrete filling between the outer stone shell and the form has "set." Now you are ready for the flue, having brought the stonework and concrete filler to this height. It is well to bury here a few of the small quarter-inch rods or heavy wire to reinforce over the drawing in of the sides.

If There Be Flues One or Many.

Now in speaking of methods of forming a flue—you can't beat the drum. If there is a good tinsmith in your neighborhood—let him make the drum. Otherwise do it yourself. A twenty-four gauge sheet of galvanized iron, tubed around wooden discs for ends, does the trick. The diameter of the top wooden disc is about one-half inch greater than the diameter of the bottom. This slight splay allows the drum to be "pulled," or slipped out easily like a cork from a bottle, after the concrete, which is poured around it is "set." Punch two holes in your top end so that an iron bar can be slipped through them to pull it out. This drum is to be wrapped around with waterproof paper of two thicknesses, tied firmly into place with string. The drum thus prepared is set into position, being the inside form of the flue. So at this point it might be wise to consider the size of the flue.

How large a flue you will need for a successful fireplace depends somewhat upon the conditions surrounding your forest home. If you are set among trees or under a high hill, you have conditions which prevent a normal "draw" and your flue must be larger than normal. With this hint I leave it to your judgment, and suggest that under ordinary conditions the area of the flue of a woods' cabin fireplace should be one-eighth of the area of the fireplace opening. Technical books will tell you that one-sixth to one-tenth is the variant—but if you make it one-eighth you have an almost condition-proof flue. Granted that this is a bit large and your flue "draws too hard" at times, you can always regulate this matter by shutting down your damper somewhat, you know. In fact, this is one of the greatest arguments in favor of a damper in a cabin. The wind and weather of the wilderness undoubtedly cause a greater variation of conditions than occurs in a town house. Usually the proud owner of an amateur-built cabin will grant you, apologetically, "Yep—it smokes in this sort of weather when the wind is this way—but it's fine other times." It would seem, in fact, that it is as much to be expected that your fireplace will smoke as that your wife will. But why not have one that will behave under all conditions? It's easy enough—if you know how. (Now—don't mistake my meaning.)

The width of the sheet of galvanized iron determines, palpably, the length of the drum—so you are going to have to draw it and set it again several times. The rock work, each time, is carried up to the height of the drum, the space between this shell and the drum is carefully filled in with concrete and left to "set." Then the drum is pulled out, rewrapped and the process repeated to the top of the stonework of the chimney. But—during this process you are gradually drawing in the diameter of your chimney both ways to avoid the appearance of clumsiness above the roof.

Obviously, in building two fireplaces into the same chimney—for instance, a dining-room and living-room fireplace—or an extra one in a bedroom for coziness—the process is the same although much more complicated. The word of caution here is to be sure to keep your flues from four to six inches apart. Very often the location of the kitchen stove makes it practicable to run the pipe through the roof. In this case, a proper sheet metal roof saddle must be used to avoid fire—and a hood should be placed atop the pipe to keep out the rains, and prevent creosote from dripping down into the kitchen.

But, in event of wishing separate flues in the fireplace chimney for the kitchen range or other stoves, you first fix upon the point at which the flue is to enter the chimney—and place the drum made to proper dimensions—eight inches in diameter—in a horizontal position entering the stonework and build the stonework up, over and around it.

As this is set, pull the drum out, reset it in a vertical position in the stonework so that it will come in juxtaposition with the horizontal flue,

Firebrick lining and arch bar.

setting the drum about six to eight inches below the bottom of the horizontal to form a pocket for soot which can be cleaned out. The reason for this is to avoid any drip of creosote down the face of the stonework.

Proceed with this kitchen flue along the same specified way, drawing it up and over the smoke chamber of the fireplace to a position paralleling the fireplace flue. In all cases, be careful to keep four to six inches away from every other flue and the smoke chamber in order that a solid concrete wall may be formed between the flues. If you wish other flues for stoves about the cabin they may be built the same way.

Flashings.

At the point where the stonework passes through the roof boarding it should be momentarily stopped at a line flush with the top of the boarding. At this point flashings should be laid in. The best is a permanent flashing of sheet lead, which is many times the cost of galvanized iron flashing but will last many lifetimes. However, very substantial flashings are sheets of twenty-four gauge galvanized iron, preferably used in full sheet and cut out to fit like a collar.

The roofing material is going on at this point and this is carried to the line of the stonework. A fresh thin layer of cement mortar is laid on the stonework, the galvanized iron being placed on this over the roofing at the lower side of the chimney and under the roofing at the upper side for a water shed, projecting into the stonework three and one-half to four inches and out over the roofing about eight inches. This over-and-under-lapping applies only, of course, where the chimney comes through at the eaves. In case the chimney goes through at the ridge, the galvanized iron lies over the roofing all around. This flashing will last for many years without painting, but a coat of paint will prolong its life and will also blend it into the coloring of the roof.

Just a hint here: You will be amply repaid for a slight delay and the cost of building paper if you cover your roof around the chimney with this paper or felt or something to keep it clean as you proceed with the messy work of your masonry. Then you will go ahead with the stonework of your chimney and feel free—if you are that kind of person—to slop your concrete all over the place.

Flashings are most important.

Flashing or "roof saddle" for stove pipe.

Chimney Cap.

When the stonework has reached the determined height of your chimney—not less than three feet above the highest point of the roof—take a look across the top of it and make sure that the stonework has been drawn in so that its outside edge is not over seven to ten inches from any point of the flue. Of course, in general, the higher the flue the better the draw—but you don't need a factory chimney. Most amateur builders err, however, in getting tired of masonic work and chopping their chimney off too soon. Having set the drums so that they project about eighteen inches above the level top of the stonework, a cement chimney cap is now built to reduce the mass to a reasonably thin edge of about three inches. This assists the air currents in pulling the smoke out. (You get the reason for this: there is a three-inch space between the opening of the flue and the outer edge of the cap.)

This cap from twelve to fourteen inches high may be built in several ways. The most satisfactory way is to build it up like a miniature stone wall, using cement and stone chips. This cement mortar is a mixture of one to two and reasonably dry—all modeled by hand. What is technically called an ogee curve—from the outside edge of the stonework to the top of the cap—makes a graceful looking finish to your masonry. (A concave curve begins at the edge of the stonework being drawn up into a convex curve at the finish.) Before this cement has set, a surfacing of about three-fourths inch thickness should be modeled over the entire face of the cap. This surfacing is a one to one mixture, and if modeled by hands covered with cheap canvas gloves, the effect is that of a sand-float finish—much more pleasing than a smooth shiny coat which has been troweled on.

Theoretically, the proper way of building a chimney cap is by utilizing small vertical rods or heavy wire mesh to reinforce the cement. These are set in the top of your chimney and you build up around them. The whole idea is to avoid a possible cracking or splitting of your chimney cap. In actual experience, however, the stone chip method described is equally satisfactory and less difficult to construct. At least, I have never heard of one that cracked or opened even after a number of years. Consequently, it seems to me that the metal reinforcement, while fool-proof, is not actually necessary.

Looking Ahead a Bit.

In the winter or any time during your prolonged absence you will find it wise to have a board cover for all of your flues to prevent leaves blowing in them, or squirrels and birds becoming squatters on your premises. To achieve a successful covering it must be fastened to your chimney in a way that will defy the wind, so—insert or bury in the cement cap four heavy copper wire loops which project about two inches above the top of the cap. Then a batten shutter or board top cut to fit the shape of the chimney with slots made in it so as to slip over these loops makes all tight when hardwood pins are thrust through the loops fastening down the cover. Another use for loops is found in attaching a wire cage to stop the sparks, if you are in a heavily timbered country where you feel that the sparks might be a menace.

This cage may be built box fashion of galvanized wire screen of one-fourth inch mesh. Don't use it unless it is really necessary, as any mesh wire will cut down the draw of your flue to a certain extent, and needs frequent cleaning.

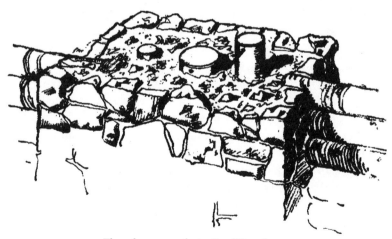

Flue-drums ready to "pull" and re-set.

Detail of chimney cap.

Placing the dome damper.

Smoke chamber built of firebrick.

The Hearth.

Now, don't forget that you still have a final bit of stonework to lay. The hearth is best put in after the roof is on, the building well along, and the finished floor laid. Previously as you pawed over your stones in making the selection for the chimney, you have laid aside your flat, colorful stones for the hearth. Now lay them out in design the way you intend to place them in the hearth. The concrete base is already in—probably about six inches below the floor. This space is to be filled with concrete grout and the selected hearthstones bedded into it and brought flush with the floor. After this operation is completed, the joints are to be filled with a one to one mixture and troweled smooth—flush with the top of the stones. Right here, one might say that while the raised hearth is preferred by many, it sometimes proves a stumbling block. In all this keep the mortar to a fairly dry mixture, as this will avoid unsightly dribble on the stones.

Detail of fireplace at "Croixsyde."

The best general caution that can be given to a novice mason is not to use everybody's advice as to how a fireplace is to be built. Some know what they are talking about; others don't—although the latter may make their suggestions sound perfectly plausible. The following true story illustrates the point: A man of good business judgment whose only short suit is ability in construction was advised to employ the days of a winter vacation in building a fireplace into his finished cabin. Discovering that the stones he had gathered were full of frost so that the cement would not work, he called together his counselors and asked what he should do about it. The wisest among them suggested that he pour kerosene over the rocks and light it—that the heat thus generated would pull out the frost. This sounded good to him and with only a minor detour he followed the line of the suggestion. Not having kerosene at hand he substituted a five-gallon can of gasoline and poured this over the pile of rocks which he had assembled inside of his cabin. He struck a match. He got out alive but since then he has left the building of fireplaces for warmer weather and other people and has been somewhat cautious about following advice.

CHAPTER ELEVEN

WINDOWS AND DOORS, CUPBOARDS AND FLOORS

In looking over assortments of windows in the vacation homes of one's acquaintances one is backed up against the wall of the conclusion that many of them were made to fit the window curtains. There is, however, what might be called an *a priori* method of selecting the style of one's windows. There are pocket windows and casement windows and windows that slide up and down or sidewise. All are available and reasonable. Which will you have? In the personal experience of building, my answer is casement windows.

Why Casement Windows?

In the first place they are much more picturesque, aren't they? They have an old-world, story-book look that seems to fit in with your primitive environment. But, of course, if you are extremely practical, this is only a by-the-way argument. What will appeal to you most is the fact that they cost less than sliding windows because they do away with counterbalance weights and sliding boxes. It is much more work to set a sliding window—this means an increase of labor. Moreover, the original cost of them is greater than that of casement windows.

Occasionally the prospective owner of a log cabin demands windows which slide sideways. The objection to these is that they are usually difficult to operate and almost impossible to make weather tight. Then there are windows which drop into a pocket, a method employed in street car windows. There are likely to use up all of your vocabulary when they stick—as they often do. Moreover, the pockets underneath the window eliminate log work which adds much beauty to the building when well fitted.

The first picture in this chapter shows Darragh Aldrich apparently writing in the southeast corner of Trailsyde. The picture was probably taken early in the history of Trailsyde, before the Crow's Nest was built as her special place for writing. Another clue about the early vintage of the picture is the lack of a large plate rack above the south window. In any restoration old photos provide clues about the development and decoration of a building. In this case I replaced the bookshelf shown above Darragh Aldrich. This faint old photo specifically shows the furniture and gives a sense of how life was conducted at the summer place.

Aldrich's comments on casement windows are out of date. With the many choices available today, there's no reason to endure drafty, balky windows. It is, of course, much to your economic advantage to buy today's standard-size windows, although the new windows often won't fit the old rough opening. For windows that are slightly larger, you need only enlarge the existing hole, but it's diffitult to disguise windows that are too small for the original opening. Custom-made windows, of course, cost significantly more.

As for trim, I try to replicate the original. Usually, however, you can save that expense. Although modern milled trim doesn't lok right in a rustic setting, you can trim off windows using three-quarter-inch-thick stock in a width proportioned to the window. Plain board looks good placed against logs. Wide board trim can mask alterations around windows, but ordinary boards are not milled to the same standard as conventional trim, so you will have to sand and finish them. The casing, windowsill, and trim should be smooth and easy to keep clean.

Baseboard trim must often be made of boards in order to bridge the space from the floor to the flat face of a log. Conventional baseboard, usually not wide enough, looks out of place, as though it belongs on a Sheetrock wall. I've occasionally used boards of eight-inch to ten-inch width for long tapers and uneven floors. An uneven floor might require that the baseboard be trimmed to five inches wide for the high areas and seven inches wide where the floor dips. You keep the top of the baseboard even as you work along the wall, but you can cheat slightly at a break in the baseboard, for example, at a doorway. A baseboard is easier to keep clean if you add a quarter-round strip on top.

Wide baseboard can sometimes hide electrical wiring. Baseboard outlets are not always permitted, however, so check with your local electrical inspector. Much electricity in log cabins was put in as an afterthought, without hiding the wire. Visible wiring stapled in place doesn't seem to bother electricians, but your cabin will look much better if you hide your wiring.

Replacing odd-size doors can be difficult. If you lack experience and shop tools, you'd probably better have a carpenter build your doors. Begin with one-by-four-inch frames doweled together and glued, with a center divider. Over one side of the frame, use paneling or boarding to complement the outside. If you plan carefully, you can cover the exterior in slabs or log siding. The frame can be insulated inside with foam sheeting. Everything attached to the frame should be glued as well as screwed or nailed. On one side you can hide all the fasteners by going through the frame. If you use three-quarter-inch stock for the faces and the frame, your door will be two-and-a-quarter inches thick, more than sufficient for a lock set. Remember to keep nails and screws away from the area where you will drill for the lock set. Use materials of appropriate thickness, or you may have to alter the casing and stops to accommodate a door that doesn't match the thickness of the original.

Later in this chapter Aldrich shows at Seven Glens a built-in cupboard with shelves and drawers. It is recessed into the wall with a log alcove projecting outside the cabin wall. You can see the exterior of the alcove in the photo captioned for shutters. The projecting alcove is very low to the ground and has minimal eave protection. These are serious flaws, but the cupboard is charming and useful. Aldrich finished the cupboard with a rich emerald-green stain lightly washed over knotty wood. The

We prefer casement windows.

In the casement window one has the advantage of a full opening. The casement sash may be hinged one upon the other in event of a very wide window, so as to fold back against the wall out of the way. This may be successfully done in any opening up to nine feet wide—thereby giving your rooms an open-porch effect. Casements are always easy to operate and can be made absolutely wind, water and air tight by utilizing a spring bronze weather strip which can be secured at a very reasonable cost.

Whether or not one should have muntins cut the sash into small panes—giving a picturesquely primitive effect—is a matter of taste. It looks well but has it disadvantages, as it not only cuts the sash but cuts the view into sections. Moreover, it is hard to keep clean. The one at which I am looking as I write has six times as many corners as if it were one light of glass. But the effect is lovely—with clean corners.

Casement sashes may be hinged one upon the other.

mellow dark knots stand out against the emerald stain, and both shades are enhanced by a coat of gloss varnish. Green stain is an Aldrich trademark, rustic but elegant. For some of his cupboards, unfortunately, he used boards with bark intact, "cull" boards that sawmills consider trash because of the bark. Stained and set in a frame, these panels look good, but the bark tends to loosen with time, and wood eating insects are attracted to the bark.

Aldrich's comments about shutters are still appropriate for any cabin in a forested area where fierce autumn storms can topple trees against a cabin. A broken window can allow considerable damage if the problem is not detected until spring. Also, it's not unheard of for a partridge to fly through a window, and you don't want to open your cabin in summer and find a decomposed bird. Although he mentions permanent hinged shutters, I'm not aware that Aldrich ever installed any himself. All of his off-season shutters were removable, for storage during the summer. Shutters not only protect the interior from natural damage but also deter winter vandals, who prefer a cabin that's not shuttered black as a cave.

Studded door of the old plank type.

Open Out Or In?

In almost any part of the country you build you are going to need screens, and casements are less easily operated if the screens are on the inside, as the screens must in this case be manipulated to be able to get at your casements or expensive and complicated hardware must be used for the sash. Moreoever, the windows when thrust out-of-doors very quickly grow dusty and streaked with rain. If they swing in, only one side is ever exposed to the weather. So if you value your hardware, paint and labor—let them swing in. As in our practical experience the casement is all around the most satisfactory, let us omit the description of other sorts. Besides, almost any carpenter will know how to put in a plain, common, double-hung window for you, and if you try to do it yourself—even following directions—you will probably have a heck of a time.

It is advisable to avoid "rabbiting" the sash at the meeting point of the stiles. Instead, use a strip of thin wood not over one-half by one and one-fourth inches screwed to one sash, forming a "strike" for the other. This scheme avoids the complications of rabbiting and simplifies the locks and hardware fastenings. The same "strip" scheme may be used to good effect on French doors.

Doors.

Without any equivocation about the matter, I am going to state dogmatically that the solid doors of a log building should not be the average factory-made doors, that is, milled doors with panels in them. They are entirely out of harmony and fling their artifice in your face as you approach. A door in keeping with the rest of the building may be made on the job, and should be a batten or plank door. In the good old days of plenty of time and lack of lumber the pioneers hewed logs into planks which were then fastened together by crosspieces called battens. These were doweled together by wooden pins driven into bored holes. This can be done now, of course, but owing to the cost of labor, the rush of life, and the lack of cunning in the hand of the workman, one never finds it. When spikes could be secured, the cross-pieces were spiked to the vertical planks top and bottom, and the nails were then clinched. The modern cabin door in imitation of this old plank door is built of two layers of boards. One layer is placed in a vertical position for one side of the door, while the boards are horizonal on the other, the nails being driven through and clinched to make it rigid. This is the simplest and easiest kind of a door to make, and if a layer of tar paper or building paper is placed between the layers of board, you have a weather-tight and bug-tight door.

A better door is made of three-ply shiplap or matched lumber of any kind obtainable. A wide shiplap, especially if of white pine and selected to contain the most sound knots, makes an extremely effective door. The white pine has "splashy" knots, and when the doors are stained, these knots take on various shades of the stain and yield a variegated effect of beautiful colors. Both sides of the door have the vertical shiplap placed over a core or center layer of horizontal. In this three-ply door, paper is not necessary.

A three-fourth inch strip of the same material is nailed or screwed to the edges of the door to cover the end wood of the horizontal layer and then planed down. This gives the door the appearance of a solid plank while it does not warp as a solid plank would be sure to do. In building this door, the parts are first of all fastened together with a few six-penny casing nails and then after the door is hung and fitted, it is actually built into rigidity by two-inch lag screws—big square-headed screws which give it the effect of an old studded door. Be sure to use enough to make all rigid—any number up to about a hundred on each side. You may think this will make your door look spotty, but take my word for it, it doesn't—especially if you are using hand-hammered hardware. Somewhat cheaper and still giving a studded effect is the old-fashioned "cut" iron nail which may be had from the larger hardware dealers. Of course, in the soft woods these do not hold so well as lag screws.

A door of similar appearance may be built of two ply shiplap, vertical on both sides, with joints lapped or "staggered." There is a three-quarter inch strip across top and bottom spiked into the boards to stiffen the door.

The doors described are heavy though in perfect harmony with the rugged effect you wish in your building. However, doors lighter in weight may be made by using matched flooring of various widths. Dresses and matched (D & M) six-inch second fencing or pine flooring, or four-inch matched spruce or fir make a good-looking door. (But in the name of all that's fitting, don't use the lumber of a city hardwood floor!) This sort of a door is made in a single layer with cross or batten strips put on in a Z or two Z form with a crosspiece bisecting the door.

If more light is needed in your room, any one of these doors may be built with a glass sash in the upper part of it. This will be found very practical in the outside kitchen door. This sash may be hinged to open, giving a window effect in the door, but more practical than this is the old Dutch Colonial door.

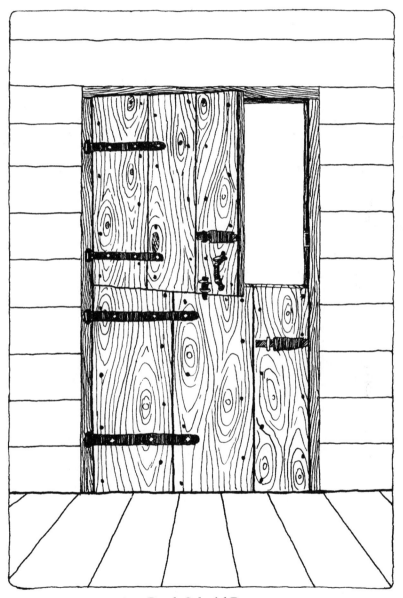

Dutch Colonial Door

The Dutch Door.

In the outside kitchen door this design will be found very useful and entirely practical as well as picturesquely quaint. Construct your door by any one of the methods above suggested and then cut it in two horizontally. At the top of the lower half fit in a small shelf four or five inches wide so that it forms a finish and a stool for the upper half of your door to strike on. Of course, the Dutch door requires an extra hinge and also extra bolts, one to bolt the two halves together and the other two to bolt each half to the frame, to keep out undesirable callers. One great advantage of the Dutch door in the kitchen is that the upper half may be open most of the time to permit the forest breezes to fan the cheeks of the cook, while the lower half is closed preventing cold drafts on the floor of the kitchen, which may ruin her baking. I have a notion that originally the Dutch doors were designed as a sort of a gate, in the days before the hooked screen was invented, to keep the small members of the large sized Dutch families where they belonged.

I don't wish to be too autocratic about this matter of doors. If you are building your own cabin and wish to have any kind of a funny door, go to it. Or you may leave it to an expert carpenter with a few suggestions as to what you want. But if you are really going in for effect, put the matter in the hands of an architect who is sufficiently interested in logs and their possibilities to be able and willing to design doors in keeping with the log work—things of beauty and a joy forever.

The French Door.

Having taken up the early American door, the studded English door and the double Dutch door, one might make the suggestion here that the French door is not out of place as long as you are going to have the doors of many nations. Especially if you are having small-paned casement windows, the French door—which is in reality only a larger casement—will be found harmonious. All glazed doors are best made at the mill and follow in general design your casements. They must be not less than two inches thick.

The convenience of cupboards, shelves and drawers.

Cupboards, Wardrobes and Shelves.

Now if you are going to have any millwork in your building, here is your chance for it, although I wish to emphasize the fact that if you are building your own cabin everything except the glass may be made by hand on the job. Appropriate doors for the cupboards are built of four- or five-inch matched flooring with batten strips. If you are really foresighted with regard to your material and have some cunning of hand as well, the thin boarding of the crates which have protected your window sash in the shipping will furnish the batten strips for all your cupboard doors as well as forming ideal material for drawers. Thus you use up what would otherwise be waste lumber. The tops of the counters above the lower cupboards are made of inch-thick dressed board. Buy several gross of screws to use in your counter tops, cupboards and other furniture, for a neater job is made thus. An expert carpenter knows all about this, but the average amateur builder forgets that screw tops may be hidden and uses nails throughout his work.

Although the usual height of a table is thirty inches, the counter top—which in a well-ordered cabin where space is at a premium substitutes for the table—is best kept to a standard height of thirty-two inches from the floor and twenty inches deep. If, however, a sink is to be established in this section, a more convenient height will be found to be thirty-six inches. If you are to have two rows of cupboards, the upper one should be raised above the counter top from sixteen to eighteen inches, thus giving you plenty of working space. In fact, two rows of cupboards will be found most convenient, as this gives one plenty of space for kneading bread or rolling out pies or piling dirty dishes. If this old-time kitchen-dresser effect is adopted, the upper cupboard is of course much shallower than the lower—being thirteen inches in the clear—and may extend to the ceiling. An effect of a more spacious kitchen is given, however, if the upper cupboard extends only to window or door height. As man to man, Comrade, let me plead of you not to use the space above the cupboards as a catch-all for old boxes, cracked dishes, and wrapping paper which you probably will never use.

"Seven Glens"—Cupboards and Doors

It is found advisable in all cupboards to have a backing of matched lumber of some sort. This makes it mouse-proof. No word of apology is needed for my assumption that these will be found regular callers, as no wilderness cabin ever existed entirely free from field mice. When you arrive in the summer, you find them sitting on the porch waiting for you to open the door, provided that in the off-season they have not been able to work out a means of access to the interior. If they have found a regularly used route, they will hop out from their nests of scrap paper and greet you at the door when you appear for your vacation. It is a well-known fact that they follow the Santa Claus trail when possible, and climb down the chimneys with their packs. In setting traps for them, by the way, don't imagine that the woods mouse cares for cheese. This is far too sophisticated bait for them, and they are extremely suspicious of it. Smear the pan of your traps with butter or lard, and you will get 'em every time!

A word about shelf-spacing may be in order here. Starting with the bottom shelf the heights which have been worked out as practical to accommodate the articles which will be probably placed in your cupboards are these: the heights of the bottom shelf sixteen inches, the next above at a space of fourteen inches, the remaining shelves twelve or thirteen inches apart. This applies to the upper cupboards, of course, as the lower cupboards will probably be used for large receptacles like old sugar tubs or the huge kettles which are found quaint and most practical in old log cabin kitchens. One shelf placed midway in your lower cupboard will be all that you need. The entire problem of heights is solved of course by making them adjustable. For this purpose, ratchets and strips may be used or a contrivance often utilized in bookcases may be purchased at almost any hardware store. This consists of a little metal bracket set into holes bored into the end walls of the cupboard.

Glass Door Cupboard

There may be places in a small kitchen where an extension counter top, hinged at the end of the cupboard, will be found convenient. This may even be used across a doorway as it can be folded out of the way.

If you have ingenuity or experienced workmen, a few drawers will be found of great advantage in your lower cupboards—especially some shallow drawers near the sink for kitchen cutlery. Perhaps an entire section of the lower cupboard space may be devoted to drawers for toweling or small kitchen equipment that is lost in a cupboard. Don't forget that while an experienced workman finds no difficulty in making and fitting a drawer, the process is rather complicated for an inexpert amateur. If the latter wishes to try his hand at it, however, let him go to work on the thin crating material before suggested for this purpose.

A beautiful rich effect for the drawer fronts may be secured by the so-called "barky" lumber—or first-run after the bark slab is taken off. This material requires some care in selection, however, as it must be taken from a log put through the sawmills soon after it was cut. Water-logged lumber or lumber which has not been properly air-cured is likely to shed the bark after a time. However, if you wish to take a chance, you will never regret the effect you have secured.

Doors for the Cupboard.

Cupboard doors may be made in several ways. Cross batten strips, or placed in Z fashion, may be screwed on or fashioned by the clinched nail method to the vertical boards. A cross strip or one-inch piece on the top and bottom edge of the door flush with the face of it may be nailed down through the vertical pieces so that no batten strips are necessary. This does not make so rigid a door, however, as the batten strips.

If one is building a more pretentious cabin and has fairly easy access to freight facilities, give your plans of the building or correct measurements of the room to the mill, stipulating that all cupboard doors are to be made with a built-up core and flush veneer facing. Experienced hands and accurate machinery will turn out a much better looking job than can be done by the amateur. In case the mill is making your cupboards, the counter tops should be built of one and one-eighth inch hardwood material with proper drain-board facility for the sink.

Bedroom Furniture—Alcove

Wardrobes and Bookshelves.

All these shelvings are built in similar manner to cupboard construction with the exception that large wardrobe doors might better be made as specified for the regular doors of the cabin. Book shelving is never over nine inches in clear, but for magazines on end the shelves must be eleven or twelve inches. If the ratchet system is used in the bookshelves, you are prepared for all comers, and "sit pretty" even if your wife pile her fashion magazines on end in 'em.

Oftentimes windows and doors come within a few inches of each other in the building. Rather than fill in this space with very small sections of logs, a construction which cuts down labor and is extremely practical is to utilize this space for small cupboards. In almost any room such a hiding place has an advantage and good use can be made of it. In the kitchen a special cupboard of this kind is found most convenient for tucking away pepper, salt and flavorings. *Cela va sans dire*—every cupboard of this kind has a flush door to hide its contents.

Wardrobes, as well as cupboards, must have a full back to make them mouseproof and also to give facilities for hanging hooks. Each one has a shelf above the hanging space, for hats, if you wear them, and a shelf may also be inserted not far from the floor as a shoe-rack. Where possible, wardrobes should be made twenty-four inches deep in the clear to allow for a crossbar accommodating clothes hangers.

The Finished Floor.

Anyone who has ever built knows that one can go the limit of expense in flooring if money is available, but beginning with the cheapest floor which looks well he will consider a material called dressed and matched six-inch second fencing. This is really a three-fourth inch board five and one-fourth inches wide with tongue and groove. Next in point of expense, is a four-inch D & M fir or spruce which is actually three-fourths inch thick by three and one-fourth inches wide. Then come the various citified hardwood floorings—all dressed and matched, of course. Of these, two and one-half inch birch is probably the least costly. From this—the expense varying inversely with the width of material—one considers the various hard woods running from two and one-half to one and one-fourth inches in width.

All of the flooring mentioned above must have an intervening insulation of heavy felt paper or a layer of tar paper with one layer of waterproof paper over it upon the rough under flooring. As suggested some time ago, tar paper is most obnoxious to bugs.

Upon this, the finished floor is laid, blind-nailed, and driven tightly together, being carefully fitted to all walls. If one uses a pine or softwood flooring, an eight-penny, cement-coated, or an eight-penny box nail will be found the best to use. In a hardwood floor, a six or eight-penny casing nail should be employed.

Although it is classed with the cheaper flooring, an eight, ten or twelve-inch wide pine shiplap is found a most effective finished floor. This is necessarily nailed directly through, with nails showing as the boards are too wide to blind-nail. However, the very fact that the nails are in evidence gives the floor a somewhat primitive look which is not undesirable.

A more expensive flooring but a very beautiful one is constructed of actual plank which is run through the mill "special" tongued and grooved. This plank may be of pine, oak, or any other material one's taste dictates and the various widths from six to twelve inches. The method of laying this floor is somewhat more complicated to gain one's effect. Holes three-fourths of an inch in diameter are bored halfway through the plank at proper intervals. Through these holes are set heavy screws which are fastened down tight to the under-floor. After the last possible twist of the screw-driver has been made, round wooden sticks or dowels of proper diameter, which can be obtained at the mill, are dipped in glue and driven into these holes—down tight onto the screw-head. The sticks are then cut off, dressed down, and sand-papered flush with the floor. This gives a wonderful reality to the old "pinned" plank floor.

In all of this discussion of finished flooring, the question will occasionally rise from the depths: Why a finished floor at all? Is not the rough board floor sufficiently rustic and artistic and all the rest of it? It is. One occasionally sees such a floor—the agony of every good housewife, for it simply cannot be kept clean. In fact, if one wished primitive effect without any other consideration entering into his choice of flooring, he might even hark back to the split pole or hewn log floor of our ancestors—and of the modern trapper's shack. An argument in favor of this is that it holds a surprise for the owner who pries it up in search of the knife or spoon which is dropped through. Underneath will be found most of the things that have been mislaid for some period as well as all articles which can be carried off by trading mice. The hewn log floor of pioneer days, however, is a most beautiful thing if well fitted and planed, but—alas for the modern hurly burly!—it is seldom found practical in point of view of labor and expense.

Casings and "Trim."

Wide casings are not in harmony with a cabin. All milled moldings which reveal the factory touch are out of keeping with the rugged effect you desire. If they are in actual fact made at the mill, great care should be taken to keep them plain and simple. Small casings of about two inches in width, merely to cover the slight joints between the log ends and frames, are best. In other words, casing has a purely utilitarian purpose—that of hiding the oakum-chinked cracks next to the window and door frames. As a consequence, the casing should be no wider than the thickness of the frame and set back one-half inch from the face of the frame. It will then project far enough back of the frame to cover the calked joint.

As a simple finish around tops of cupboards and wardrobes, a three-fourth inch strip of board is found sufficient. Where in a city home moldings are utilized, the plain strip will be found not only adequate in a cabin but much more in keeping with the idea of primitive simplicity.

Without Doubt You Will Have Screens.

One may take it for granted that screens will be extremely necessary wherever one builds. On the shores of good old Lake Superior we do not suffer from mosquitoes, but there is the ever present fly. Deer flies, horse flies, fish and personal flies. All of these are voracious, rapacious. Hence, screens. It is almost impossible for any ordinary mesh of screen to be a protection against the very small gnats and "No-see-ums." (If you have never made the acquaintance of the latter, you don't know what real discomfort is.) There may not be a fly in the neighborhood, but any culinary attempt will draw them out of the ether. They materialize into being above a pan of frying fish, for example, in a way that outdoes the most conscientious effort of a spiritualistic medium. Let this be sufficient argument for window and door screens. Then, if you have a front porch for gossipy rocking chairs or for shelling peas, you will undoubtedly want it screened. This is most conveniently done in sections. Panels of wire mesh are made like large window screens and fitted in between the pillars of your porch. As long as you must freight in your window sash, you may as well freight in your screens which can be made for you at the mill. While it is more than possible to ship the screening by roll and the tacks by the pound, it is much more expensive in the end to make the screens on the job.

There are practically only three sorts of wires among which to choose—the cheapest being common black iron wire, twelve wires to the inch or twelve mesh. Unless otherwise specified, the mill will use this. A coat of black screen paint must be given at once to keep this in condition—the operation being repeated every two or three years thereafter. A thin coat of creosote oil applied every year is a fairly good substitute for the black paint. Consequently, if you are taking into account the cost of labor, or your expenditure of personal effort, this cheaper screening ultimately totals the original cost of a more expensive wire, which requires less upkeep. In point of expense, we arrive next at "pearl" wire, which is a galvanized fourteen mesh wire. It is a so-called non-rust wire, but this adjective is not absolutely accurate.

The more expensive wires—but ideal in that they need no paint at any time—are copper and copper bronze wires with a standard sixteen mesh. From this standard it increases to a very fine mesh that not only keeps out gnats but also the curious gaze of the neighbors and passers-by. This wire cloth is almost rain-proof, except in the case of wind-driven storms, and is actually non-rustable. When purchased, the copper is bright, but oxidizes in time so that the standard mesh is almost an imperceptible medium between the eye and the surrounding landscape.

The easiest and simplest fastenings for screens are two or two-and-a-half-inch brass—or galvanized iron—hooks and eyes. With these your screens are easily set into place when you arrive, and removed in a jiffy when you go. (It is assumed, of course, that you are thrifty enough to remove your screens and pack them away for next season.)

Shutters.

Shutters may be merely a rough protection, during the off season, against prowlers or the falling of trees or the breaking of limbs in storms. Then, too, one must take into consideration that wandering hunters often have a very bad aim which may shatter window glass, and that small boys have a most excellent aim and love crashing noises. Hence, shutters.

The removable shutter may be made of matched lumber such as flooring if you don't care for the looks of rough boards. Either smooth or rough, the vertical boards are made rigid with batten strips top and bottom. These shutters are fastened on the inside to the window frames, after the screens have been removed, with four to six small hasps and hardwood pins. (Clothes pins are an excellent substitute.) Hooks and eyes will fasten the shutters but are not prowler-proof. Instead of screwing the hasps onto the shutters, a preferable way is to nail them on and clinch the nails. Then bring on your darn old housebreakers.

Shutters of a permanent type may be hinged to the building. These are most practical if you don't mind hiding such large sections of the log work when they are swung back. (Well-fitted logs—to the mind of one who loves 'em—constitute the chief beauty of the building.) The shutters may be hinged to the building in pairs, opening up like double doors, or one upon another and folded back out of the way. The advantage of the permanent type of shutter is that it takes less time to open up the building when you arrive—a great point in their favor—with a week-end occupant. These require additional hardware, of course, not only in hinges but contrivance to hold them open—and shut.

Your cabin should be shuttered when you leave.

CHAPTER TWELVE

PORCHES, TERRACES AND BALCONIES

As we inferred before, the pioneer cabin had no porch because pioneers had no time to sit on it. Despite the proverbial rush of the present day, we do have time for porches—especially when taking vacations. Your ideal cabin springs up naturally amid its setting and the porch adds greatly in achieving this effect. As the colonnade of trees leads to the entrance of your home, so this—if it be a porch especially—leads to the more intimate shelter of your hearth. Let there be no jarring note.

Long ago you planned your porch along with the plan of the cabin, and when you began building, the sill logs of the porch were built into the stonework of your foundation or locked into the logwork of the whole structure. Porch floor joists may be either the small logs of your supply or 2x8's or 2x10's. If the joists are the round small logs, hewn on top and leveled as specified for the main building, stability demands that they be placed not over twenty-four inches apart, as your porch will have only a single floor. The joists are set at a one-inch pitch away from the building to carry off the rain. If the "two-bys" are used, sixteen inches is a sufficient distance between them. The floor will be the same material as the finished floor of the building. Whether or not it is set flush with the floor of the building or dropped somewhat below it is a matter of individual choice. If your young folks need an added space for dancing, or if you plan on using it as a dining porch, it will be found more convenient to have it flush with the main floor. Otherwise the porch may be dropped two inches to allow for door sill. Moreover, when the contour of your ground slopes away from the front of your building—as almost invariably happens in the case of a lake-shore

One of my fondest log-cabin memories is of the venerable Boy Scout camp Many Point. Russel Gaylord built the original cabin there in the days when powerful men of industry had elaborate hunting camps along the duck and goose flyways. Gaylord's camp, however, was slightly off the main flyway, and eventually the property came into the hands of the Scouts, who added handsome log buildings, with Gaylord's lodge remaining as the crown jewel.

Gaylord's lodge is large and two-storied with a magnificent porch wrapped around three sides. The porch begins as part of the kitchen on one side. It continues across the front of the building, in a wide screened expanse that holds an ample assortment of comfortable old chairs and convenient tables, and then around the other front corner, terminating in a closed bedroom or gameroom. On a warm afternoon, one of life's pure pleasures is to sit on that porch, feet propped on a rail, and watch the lake, where you can hear happy boys in the distance. (Often the best way to enjoy boys is from a distance, especially if you've spent the day working with them.)

Aldrich would have liked that porch, since he doted on porches in general. Nevertheless, porches present problems. In Aldrich's day, in order to look inviting the porch had to be informal, and sometimes informality came at the expense of solid construction. Seven Glens, for example, changes roofline from cabin roof to porch roof, forming a valley, and changes again in less than five feet, where a purlin creates a second valley, in order to reduce the pitch of the roof and gain headroom. It's quaint, woodsy, picturesque, and charming. But multiple valleys on low-pitched roofs are forever given to leaking.

For the sake of looks, Aldrich often sacrificed practicality, for example, with shaggy cedar. Insects settle in with you when you retain the bark

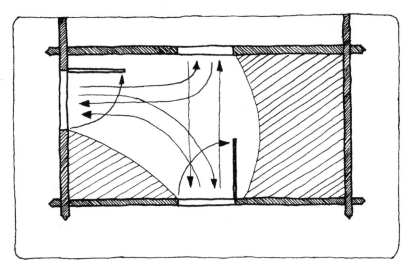

Original Aldrich Plan

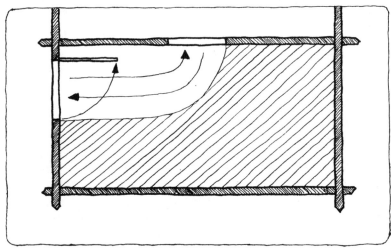

Improved Porch Plan
Discussed on p. 34.

frontage—it not only adds picturesqueness to the interior but allows the exterior to conform with the lines of your ground, producing an effect of your cabin snuggling down into its setting if you drop the porch floor one or two steps below the main floor. I know of one instance in which such a difference in levels gives to a most attractive living room the effect of a stage setting when viewed from the porch.

Just a word about your roof-line by the way. If your cabin is of the smallest variety and if possible—which means if the level is practicable—have your porch roof an extension of your main roof. If this would mean that you bumped your fool head each time you crossed the porch, flatten the pitch of your porch roof. The average cabin porch looks like a barnacle on a ship's side. Just keep in mind the fact that this ante-room is an honest-to-goodness integral part of the house itself, not a makeshift or an afterthought. Accent the "log" part all you want—but make it a "loggia" not an "apologia."

For your porch posts you have selected your best large logs—not forgetting that a well-known optical illusion reduces the actual diameter of vertical posts. This does not mean that they are to be very massive, but certainly you will wish them to look substantial.

Shaggy cedar bark is beautiful for columns and unless there has been undue demand for railroad ties in your forest neighborhood, you are likely to be able to corral some lovely specimens for the porch posts. Remember one thing in selecting: cedar which has met its end bravely standing—or in the phrase of your unpoetically precise woodsman, has "died on the butt"—is especially inclined to be retentive of its bark and is therefore the most desirable for your purpose.

At the height of the plate log of the porch you again build into the log wall of the main structure for rigidity, carrying up the gable ends of the porch in a manner precisely similar to that described in building the gables of the house. The rafters for the porch are set in like manner to those of the main building, and, if the porch is wide, there should be a purlin log as in the main roof for an extra support under the center of the rafter. If the porch is very long, the long purlin may again be supported by level logs extending from each post back to the building, a short strut from these supporting the purlin. The rafters are cut into the plate logs of the porch in the same fashion as in the building, the upper end of the rafter being housed or built into the main wall. As the rafter ends are ax-cut, plenty of length must be allowed for this and for a goodly projection of the porch roof. These porch eaves afford not only protection from the weather but grace the building with a sort of quaint beauty. Of course, the whole projection depends upon the size of the porch, but it is never less than twenty inches from the outside face of the plate log to the edge of the roof boarding. Sometimes in a large building a three-foot projection will not be overdoing the matter. For the porch boarding and roofing, follow the specified details of the same construction in the main building. Seldom is a double roof for insulation used on a porch.

A very important point is the tight flashing where a porch roof joins the building below the main roof. Long strips of galvanized iron six to ten inches in width may be lapped on to the log work for three or four inches and then bent at the critical line to extend out upon the roofing. Before this is nailed into place, it is best to give the underside of your flashing a light coat of the pitch which comes with the roofing. Thus are you insured against any weather. Manifestly, the upper edge of the flashing will be hammered to hit the contour of the log and fastened with galvanized shingle nails placed an inch apart along the strip. A regular roofing nail fastens it through the roofing at the lower edge. After all is in place, paint the galvanized iron the color of the roofing.

Railings or Not?

Some people prefer their porches screened to the floor, with the effect of colonial pillars between the wire panels, but if your porch is utilitarian as well as esthetic, it is usually preferable to have a railing—open or sheathed. If it is open, the screens extend down behind it to the floor. If it is sheathed, matched boarding is fitted from the railing to the floor and the screen panels are set in above the rail. Although the height of the railing is, of course, optional, it might be noted here that the standard height is two feet six inches. If you have elected to use the sheathed railing, the lower panel of your porch screen door should also be solidly sheathed for conformity's sake.

Now I beg of you not to fall into conventional rusticity in the matter of the railings. The use of bent or crooked limbs of trees criss-crossed in a weak-kneed sort of fashion has been done to death. It ought never to have been started. Design something that fits your building and give some slight indication of your sense of the artistic. Many lovely lines may be obtained with small saplings of two or three inches in diameter—straight and true. Another type of railing but more expensive because of greater labor may be fashioned of hewn balusters.

on wood, especially untreated exposed wood. The open porch shown with a split-pole roof is on the Crow's Nest, and I can assure you that the shaggy bark railings are history. The bark was colonized by bark beetles long ago, and the open porch and rough ceiling became a haven for insects and bats. The porch should have been screened off to deter vermin and also make the porch space more useful. Aldrich claims there was no mosquito problem along Lake Superior's north shore, but I've stood on that porch in a haze of mosquitoes that gathered under the shady overhang with me.

You're better off with a glazed porch that can be warmed in cool weather. The porches in Aldrich's sketches in this chapter would be improved by replacing the open screens with screen-and-window units. Of course, there's no sense in adding costly window units if the porch has suffered so badly from the elements that it needs rebuilding from floor to roof. Examine the soundness of the whole before deciding on windows.

Aldrich's stoop idea is rather good, but as far as I know Aldrich used it only on Totem Pole Lodge, where the stoop decayed because it rested on the ground. I have added a stoop to Trailsyde, following Aldrich's lines and materials. My woodwork does not rest on the ground: the base and stoop floor are concrete, leaving exposed the aggregate of Lake Superior beach gravel. My screened stoop is small, but it provides some firewood storage and helps keep the cabin clean, because the stoop catches much of the debris tracked in by boots and shoes. I think Aldrich would approve of both the idea and its execution.

The picture illustrating Aldrich's comments on terraces is a view of the west side of Squantum. From this view you'd think Squantum's low-pitched roof was horizontal. Maurice Maine, Squantum's designer and primary builder, planned to add a bedroom on the terrace, with access through one of the two doorways, while the other doorway would still open onto the remainder of the terrace. Squantum was never expanded, however, partly because the design was flawed by the same low roof pitch that plagued Aldrich's cabins.

All sorts of individual effects are gained by a fancy in design of the balustrade or by a grouping of the pillars instead of having them spaced regularly. A cabin of which I wot has an interesting shelter formed by the roof's extension, supported by posts in groups of three direct to the ground itself and placed far enough in to give wide eaves. It gives a very definite and interesting impression of the Japanese. The simplest and probably the most "cabinish" way to build your porch is to extend the gable end, chalet-fashion, and support it by pillars. From both views—inside and out—this is unusually satisfactory, especially upon a small cabin.

In the Studio Cabin this effect is enhanced a lot by the roof of split poles, carefully matched and placed by a real craftsman at log work.

The Glazed-In Porch.

Wind and storm in certain localities demand a glazed-in porch for comfort's sake. This can be achieved most easily and artistically by utilizing the regular casement sash either in pairs, hinged one on the other, or in series of larger sash hinged at the top to lift up and hook to the ceiling out of the way. If expense, time and labor are not items of great moment to you, pockets may be built for the sash to drop into, but remember that this sort of thing is complicated to build and to operate. Of course, in your glazed porch you will have your doors glazed too.

As to porch steps, the simplest as well as the most artistic and easiest to make have plank sides with half logs for treads. Extremely effective steps are built of split stones left over from the fireplace.

If You Like Terraces.

It may be that a terrace will appeal to your artistic soul more than the somewhat conventional porch. The true terrace is open, but a good effect is achieved by roofing, or you may arrange a pergola of logs and poles. This then is rather an open porch than a terrace. In fact, it may be a porch as far as its usability is concerned, but its floor will have a more picturesque appearance as it is made of slab rock—so-called flagstones. Where a stone foundation is used in the building, it is best to make your terrace of stone—an effect which is not infrequently found at old New England farm-houses. If you are in a slate country, keep in mind that slab slate—even the waste material—makes the finest possible terrace flagging.

Waste stone, too, uneven odds and ends, may be found at a stone mill, and these yield the loveliest effect imaginable in your terraced floor.

If you like terraces.

Open Porches or "Stoops."

At the kitchen door you will need some sort of a platform—preferably covered—for convenience sake. Here will be found extra wood, water pails, your washing bench—all sorts of things—dependent upon how primitive you plan to be. Although the Dutch "stoep" has its points, in our native land where rains abound it is far more sensible to have a roof over your platform. From this, as a minimum protection, you may have anything you wish even to a screened porch off your kitchen. When the season is likely to be extremely warm, the latter will be found very convenient to use as a sort of out-of-door kitchen.

When You May Choose a Balcony.

However much your artistic soul may yearn for a balcony, picturing your Romeo self gazing upward at your fair Juliet above, don't try to tack it onto a small building. In fact, there is no reason or beauty in a balcony attached to other than a two-story (at least a story and a half) building. However, if the dimensions of your structure permit this addition to beauty, space and convenience, have a balcony by all means. Proportion should be your main consideration in designing it. The maximum, for instance, is about half the width of your building, and it should center your elevation for symmetry's sake. In general, it is more effective placed at the end of the building. It is best supported by real constructional logs which are cross-wall logs carried through and projecting outside the building. Or it may be supported by log joists projected through the building. Any of these logs, in order to conform to the other projecting logs of the building, will have ax-cut ends and are coped—either being bolted together or fastened with lag screws. In constructing your balconies in this way, brackets will not be found necessary but, if for any reason this method of building cannot be carried out, a log bracket support must be used.

A single flooring of dressed plank set about a quarter of an inch apart to allow for drainage, forms the floor.

There are many types or designs of railings—open or sheathed as you will. If the balcony is used as an auxiliary sleeping porch, common sense dictates the sealed railing. Probably the most useful and artistic is the semi-closed railing, formed of vertical boards five or six inches wide, dressed and "cut out" upon the edge in various designs. This gives you the effect of a Swiss balcony.

Now, if you are going to have a balcony, keep it a balcony. Don't try to roof it and screen it and turn it into a hanging sleeping porch. In the latter case, you hardly need even a cuttle fish bone stuck through the wire to suggest a bird cage. Make up your mind whether you want a screened porch or balcony and build accordingly.

In order not to be dogmatic, let me say here that balconies may be of so many types, sizes and uses that—aside from these general hints—it is futile to try to describe them further or to give more specific directions for their construction. Make sure that the whole thing is sound—that the railings are firmly fixed to the floor and tied into the building in substantial fashion. Stability here may be secured by bolts, lag screws, or strap iron. As this hardware is exposed to the weather, they should be either galvanized iron or black iron treated with oil to prevent rust streaks down your building.

Plenty of room for dancing.

Used as a sleeping porch, it is screened to the sealed railing.

Shaggy cedar makes the porch of "Crow's Nest."

CHAPTER THIRTEEN

IN WHICH ARE DISCUSSED VARIOUS ITEMS OF HARDWARE

It is mainly a question of your pocket-book whether you will use hand-made hardware throughout your building or stock hardware throughout or hand-made hardware in part of it and stock hardware in part. There are several nationally known shops in the country which, at a considerable expense to yourself, will supply all of your hardware, really hand-made, in designs that will rejoice your soul. Then there is the oft-mentioned village smithy, or if you are fortunate enough to be near an old deserted logging camp, you are likely to find there, going to pot, the product of a beautiful art wrought by a real artist at the forge. I do not wish to suggest that you relieve any great-hearted lumber company of this neglected treasure for a sample of what may be wrought, but take along your screwdriver and some handy prying tool and do as your conscience bids you.

The usual camp's "forge artist" learned his trade in the old country through a four- to six-year apprenticeship. His title was "blacksmith," but this did not indicate merely shoeing of horses. He was capable of making everything in a logging camp that could be made of iron—from a nail to the full iron equipment of sleds and wagons. Chains, hooks for the doors—hinges and latches for the buildings. Upon all these he practiced his artistry. I saw once a rose fashioned of iron that one of these smiths wrought in his spare time. It was a lovely thing, and who shall say that this was not a chef d'œuvre worthy of a Salon placing?

But to come back to the discussion of your hardware, there is a factory putting out at a reasonable cost such an excellent imitation of the old hand-made hardware that few will detect the difference.

This chapter on hardware is barely useful today, when hardware choices are vastly different. Some shops specialize in reproduction hardware or in salvage hardware from old houses. In many cases, though, the choices will be limited to what is in vogue, such as Colonial and Victorian.

Early in the chapter Aldrich shows windows with black iron hardware with an emphasis on simplicity. In this picture, notice the view of the ceiling. There are many small gaps where the rafters fit into notches in the top log, where the purlins poke through the gable ends, and where the roof boards and logs meet. Those openings were usually plugged with oakum or caulk, and as long as the cabin had an open ceiling, it was possible to keep an eye on such caulking. With a ceiling added, however, you have a whole new adventure in disaster.

The open ceiling was home to the occasional spider, whereas an added false ceiling creates a spacious mouse apartment. Lumberyard salesmen claim that mice won't nest in fiberglass. But mice don't know that. Sooner or later a ceiling added to a rustic building has to be removed or replaced. The mice chew up the insulation, reducing its effectiveness, and the only way to keep mice out is to start over and do it right. I won't describe the particular joys of pulling down old ceilings. Wear a dust mask, eye protection, and clothes you don't care about. Don't look too closely at what falls out of the ceiling as you work.

Even after you've removed the ceiling debris, you've still got a big cleaning job. In their protected overhead home, the mice have gnawed wood and built a mouldy larder, so the uncovered ceiling is rough and ugly.

Before painting, wire-brush and scrub the wood and caulk or putty the board gaps, cracks, and holes. If you've decided to leave your purlins and rafters natural or contrasting, give them a good scrub and a fresh coat of varnish. Clean and varnished, these pieces will not allow paint to stick as easily, so after you paint the roof boards, cleanup will be easier. If your boards have survived reasonably well, you may be able to skip the painting and retain the cabin's old look of natural log rafters and purlins set against mellow pine roof boards. Although this treatment elminates overhead insulation, it also eliminates a haven for rodents.

The following technique allows you to retain the exposed pole rafters while hiding badly damaged overhead boards and adding some insulation above. First glue and fasten sheets of styrofoam insulation to the boards in the spaces between the pole rafters. Over the insulation, glue sheetrock and fasten it with sheetrock screws. Sheetrock mud gives a tight joint where sheetrock and rafters meet.

Mice will not bother this construction too much, especially if you use the dense foil-covered styrofoam, instead of the loose beadboard form. You can make barriers of hardware cloth tacked around the perimeter and in any other trouble spots you notice. If there are gaps that extend toward the outside, fill them with hardware cloth and apply caulk thoroughly. Pay attention to the ridge area: nearly all rodents are excellent climbers, and squirrels in particular like to enter by a peak or ridge.

Another technique insulates the roof from outside without disturbing the interior look. Put styrofoam over the old roof, add plywood over that, and then install new roofing. But you must be careful and meticulous. I know of more than one cabin that leaks mouse-gnawed styrofoam like artificial snow.

Insulating the roof provides mixed benefits. An uninsulated roof allows the sun to warm the whole building, although you have to use supplemental heating on chilly days. If your cabin is seldom used in cool weather, then you may prefer to skip overhead insulation. An uninsulated roof also avoids problems of venting and vapor barriers. Styrofoam, especially foil-faced, doesn't absorb much humidity, but many other insulating materials do, and they therefore require venting and vapor barriers. Consider the potential condensation problems beforehand. A cabin that can't breathe will decay. Mold and mildew, forming like black

Black iron is effective in hardware.

Black iron seems best to harmonize with the rugged log buildings, and this sort of hardware has the advantage of being less costly as well. Set against any color scheme that you may choose for your interior decoration—or against the logs themselves—it proves very effective.

Though considerable time and labor in finishing the woodwork may be saved by setting locks, latches and bolts after this finishing is done, all hinges must be put on the windows and doors before you apply your varnish, stain or oil, as these must be hung and properly fitted first.

Hinges.

On the casement windows a light strap hinge of any of the many designs is fitting and artistic. More practical is the regular butt hinge cut into the edge of the sash and jamb of the frame. In connection with this, however—if you wish to keep the old-time effect of the strap—metal plates may be applied to the sash which represent the various designs of the old-time hinge. You may find that the plain butt hinges are sufficient in themselves, obviating the extra cost of the metal application, as curtains or side drapes are likely to hide this portion of the sash anyhow. If you have French doors, a plain heavy butt hinge is the simplest to use.

The most practical hinge for a heavy door is the screw-pin and strap-hinge which is now obtainable from most hardware dealers in a regular stock of all sizes from four inches to four feet. The pin looks like a turned-up round iron hook that screws into the door frame and has a shoulder for the strap to rest upon. The strap is formed from a flat iron bar bent around an up-turned pin and doubled back on itself part way. Holes being bored through the strap at intervals permit its being bolted to the door. Again with an eye for proportion—the average cabin door being two feet eight to three feet wide, and six feet to six feet eight high (or seven if you are likely to have tall guests) the best appearance is given by three hinges. Two straps of about sixteen inches in length are placed on the door—one about six inches below the top of the door, the other nine or ten inches up from the bottom—and a third one, of slightly less length, halfway between these two. This same scheme of hinging may be utilized on French doors for uniformity's sake, although the center hinge will not be over five inches in length, as this is the width of the door stile. A plain straight strap-hinge of about a quarter-inch thickness is the regular stock size which may be purchased, and an effect of hand-work may be given by having your village smithy hammer this out into some shape of individual fancy. If you wish to go into more detailed designs of the hand-made variety, then the strap-hinge must be selected from one of the excellent catalog designs of the various well-known forges—or made special for you.

If you insist on being strictly sophisticated in your building, and wish a double swing or flap-door between kitchen and dining-room, the hardware merchant will supply you with three double-acting spring hinges, provided you give him the size and thickness of the door.

If you have a Dutch door, the four strap-hinges should be of the same length. A screw-pin and strap-hinge should be used on your screen door to conform with the others but in a smaller size—probably an eight-inch length.

Of course, you will hinge your skylight, and a stock T-hinge may be used here. At this point it might be well to note that a hinged skylight may be operated in any one of a number of ways. You will find probably, on looking out-of-doors, that a tree has thoughtfully placed itself so that a pulley may be fastened on it about two feet above the height of your

soot on the woodwork, signal a serious moisture problem that must be cured.

The three-room cabin sketched in this chapter is Seven Glens. Aldrich shows a bed in the room immediately behind the fireplace, but with the limited space and the plethora of doors, it seems an unsatisfactory bedroom. In the porch at the bottom of the sketch, the dashed lines indicate the purlin that creates another valley in the roof. In the photo you can see that the eave edge of the roof is almost horizontal, even with the porch two steps down. The cupboard alcove discussed in chapter 11 can be seen jutting from the wall of the main room. The many jogs in the walls made this cabin difficult to build. Despite some practical flaws, Seven Glens has character, which perhaps explains why Aldrich shows this plan often.

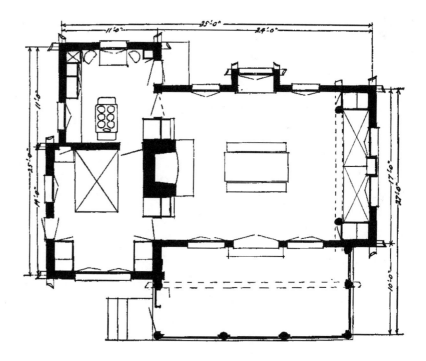

Plan of three-room cabin.

skylight. In this case, a second pulley four or five feet up from the floor is fastened to the wall outside, and a rope attached to the skylight is run through these two pulleys and brought through a hole bored in the log wall. Thus it may be operated from inside the cabin. The good old logging-camp style of operating a skylight from within is by a notched stick.

Hinges for the cupboards and wardrobes are practically the same as the window hinge—an ordinary butt hinge cut into the door and jamb or applied directly to the faces thereof. If this latter surface method is selected, it is better to use a light T-hinge.

Bolts and Catches.

We have experimented with all sorts of mortised bolts to fasten the sash tight, and after long experience have come to the conclusion that the surface bolt is most practical. Each set of sash should have a turn-buckle or fastener upon the central meeting stiles. Where the sash are hinged one on another, or in banks, a metal pull should be placed on the meeting stiles to facilitate their handling. This metal pull may be much like a drawer handle.

On cupboards, each pair of doors is equipped with a cupboard "turn" or catch placed usually on the right-hand door of each pair, an elbow catch on inside of the left-hand door. A fastener for this catch placed on one of the shelves will then make the doors behave themselves. In ordering hardware, if you do not choose to have drawer handles of wood—hand-made by yourself and screwed on from the inside of the drawer —you may order metal pulls for them along with the rest of the hardware. On the windows it is advisable to put surface bolts at the top as well as the bottom of the sash.

Latches.

The hardware which holds the greatest possibilities of beauty as well as utility is found on the doors. A knob should never be used in a log building. Its place is taken by the thumb-latch. In the cheaper hardware there are many stock patterns in pressed steel among which to choose, but again the most fitting is the hand-wrought latch hammered out by the village blacksmith or selected from the fine Colonial designs of hand-made latches found at the exclusive New England forges. There is in a latch also an imitation of the hand-hammered work which may

Strap hinges on a French door.

be had at reasonable cost. In our interesting collection of latches, one of the most artistic is made from a common round iron bar—hammered into beauty by a lumber-camp blacksmith.

In setting the latch, the bar of the thumb-piece might well be in line with the central hinge of the door—which generally brings it about three feet from the floor.

Occasionally, one may wish in addition to the latch, some sort of a bolt to insure privacy. This should be a sliding surface bolt. On French doors it will be found well to place two of these bolts—which are about eight or ten inches long—one at the top and one at the bottom of each of the pair of doors.

When it come to the question of locking your outside doors—if you are festive enough to have more than one—all may be bolted from the inside except one. This may be fitted up with a mortised tumbler lock or night-latch tumbler lock. If you prefer something more primitive, a most effective fastening, both from the point of view of art and utility, is a hasp and substantial padlock. At Wa-wa-tay Post, a building which I constructed as game and forestry headquarters of Minnesota, there are padlocks of such a notable size that they call for the loud expressions of marvel and delight from the casual visitor.

While we are chatting of wrought-iron hardware, the fireplace crane comes in for a special word. This may be had in a choice of several designs from dependable dealers, but here again is offered an opportunity for one's individual fancy. Tell your friend, the smithy, the proper measurements and let him see what he can do for you. Be sure to give him the number of inches from top of lug to top of lug, as they are set in your fireplace, as well as the width of the latter.

Poker and tongs of black iron are mighty useful around the fire, and these, too, may be purchased, factory-made of stock designs, or fashioned by the smithy according to a gracious composite of your ideas and his own. If you have firedogs, it is almost necessary to have them specially designed and made to fit your fireplace, as none of those which I have discovered on the market seem to be harmonious with a log building. They should be exceedingly sturdy looking and lack any attempt at fancy designing—at least to my mind. Most successful firedogs are made from old sixty or seventy pound steel rails discarded from an abandoned railroad. If you have the luck of discovering something like this, have the rail cut in lengths just the depth of your fireplace. At a distance of five inches from the front end of each piece, cut away the flange and lower web. The upper member is then turned up like a sled runner—thus preventing the logs from rolling out. These iron dogs raise the logs up from the floor of the fireplace, giving a circulation of air beneath and prepare for a corking fire.

CHAPTER FOURTEEN

FINISHING THE LOGS AND THE WOODWORK

Of course, it is not necessary to do anything at all with your logs and your woodwork. Pioneer cabins had no finish but that provided by the weather. Leave everything alone and let nature take its course. This is the simplest and most unsatisfactory way. It all depends on what kind and how much weather you have. In very moist climates, the wood will take on deep hues in time. It will even turn black. If you think your great-grandchildren wish this sort of thing, leave the finish of your cabin to the weather. Weathering may be done very carefully, however, with great success. A small cabin which I built for our State Historical Society as an exact replica of the early pioneer cabin in our Northwest was originally put up out-of-doors and no treatment given the logs or woodwork. After two years it was taken down, piece by piece, and then assembled and set up in the museum exhibition rooms. The weather had turned it a lovely silver gray.

The next step away from the primitive is found chiefly in southern plantations where the cabins were whitewashed inside and out. This certainly helped to preserve the logs and if you wish that sort of cabin—go to it. I have found, however, that people of the present day who build with logs want the newness of the wood somewhat preserved and thus add beauty of coloring to beauty of design in their cabins.

Oiling.

Woodwork and logs may be treated in so many ways that it comes finally to be a matter of individual taste.

Many of my clients wish nothing but a finish of oil on the entire

Aldrich liked dark colors. His deep brown floors are gloomy, almost dirty looking. Some of his cabin floors have been stripped, revealing the natural pine, which can be varnished. Stripping such floors makes the cabin brighter, but for harmony with the past I avoid wholesale changes to the tones and schemes popular now. I think a cabin should retain some of its original character as a reflection of bygone days and other people. In a careful examination of your cabin's era, you will find plenty of authentic color schemes and designs for decoration and blending. Some of today's finishes are not compatible with the old oil-based finishes, so experiment with test areas in case the old and new formulas collide like vinegar in milk. I corrected one abused floor in the bathroom of an Aldrich cabin by first covering the entire floor with a new layer of quarter-inch waterproof plywood, glued and screwed over the original floor. I filled all the joints, gaps, and areas around pipes with water putty or filler, which I sanded smooth after drying. The screw holes, too, had to be filled, much as you'd do with Sheetrock or plaster board. I gave the new plywood floor several coats of sealer. The smooth, sealed floor then became the base for a decorated canvas floor. A canvas floor offers all sorts of opportunities for personalized decoration. I used stencils to create a border of green pines with dark brown trunks. Some people like to incorporate the name of the cabin into a central design. Additional ideas on canvas floors can be found in books about early American interiors. Canvas rugs and floors are part of our folk-art traditions.

Tan and natural off-white canvas are commonly available in preshrunk

bathroom-size pieces. As you lay out the canvas over the sealed ply-wood, don't stretch your canvas, because uneven pulls will show. You have to work and trim slowly. Start with the longest wall and tack the canvas close to the wall. Where a pipe goes through the floor, you'll have to slit the canvas. When the entire canvas floor is down, trimmed, and tacked, apply a coat of varnish diluted thirty percent with thinner. Stencil with a compatible paint (oil-based paint for oil-based varnish), and then give the decorated floor two coats of varnish. Cover the tacked edges with baseboard or quarter round and install a brass threshold in the doorway. Use escutcheon rings to dress up and conceal areas around pipes. The resulting floor is both personalized and durable.

Aldrich shows a drawing of a substantial hunting and fishing lodge from New Brunswick, but I do not know if it was built. This lodge has distinct Aldrich touches such as the style of the chimneys.

building—logs, outside and in, floors, doors and window sash. This simple linseed oil treatment preserves the wood and mellows it in color. It prevents it from turning grey or black from the weather and keeps it to the lighter tints of orange, yellow and tan which are particularly effective in logs.

When the whole matter is left to my own discretion, I make sure that the logs are peeled clean in the first place and, either as the building is going up or after it is finished, I begin work on the logs outside and in. Three coats of boiled linseed oil are applied warm: the first coat is about twenty per cent turpentine, the second coat ten per cent and the third coat the clear oil. Of course, plenty of time must be left between coats, for it takes from a few days to two weeks for this finish to soak in and dry. The purpose of the turpentine is to assist in "striking" or setting the oil in the woodwork. A precautionary word about heating oil: Don't get it so hot as to curl your brush, and don't think when it begins to agitate in the pail on the stove that it is boiling. It is merely beginning to warm up and should be tested by your finger. When it is as hot as you can stand it, take it off the stove and add turpentine. Never mix the turpentine and oil first and then try to heat it, as turpentine around a fire is an extreme hazard.

This oil finish should be applied with a four- or five-inch flat brush, taking care not to splash it on. Don't dip the brush too deep into the oil—and brush it well into the log work as you go along.

If You Like Color.

One person likes a colorful cabin—another doesn't. As you choose. You may be as brilliant as you like, provided you use judgment in selecting colors that harmonize with each other and are not out of place in a forest setting. Various shades of brown and green will not be found incongruous.

In any event, if you have decided on color, the coloring pigments are put into the first coat of oil and turpentine and mixed to the approval or satisfaction of whoever is dictating the matter. Colors ground in oil are utilized. (This technical term means simply that you purchase them in paste instead of in dry form.) The coloring mixture should be thin enough to be of the nature of a stain rather than of a paint. In this way, the beauty of the grain of the wood is retained, and the knots yield a lovely, variegated effect. There are many prepared stains on the market which may substitute for the hand-made mixture; but one should experiment with these to make sure that they are precisely what one wants. Of course, if nobody raises an objection to the odor of creosote around the building for several months, there are some good creosote stains to be had. However, unless you have some expert to dictate for you, such as an architect who knows logs and how to treat them, it is best to experiment first on waste pieces of board and log before doing anything serious in your building.

This possibility of staining in various colors applies not only to log work but to all woodwork: ceiling, floors, sash, posts or balusters—everything. Remember that a log which is merely peeled will probably not take on any color as there is a film of sap left on the outside surface of the peeled log which prevents the stain from taking effect. This is particularly true of spruce and balsam. Somewhere back near the beginning of things, I suggested that if you were looking forward to coloring your logs, they must be draw-shaved well into the surface of the wood.

As inferred pretty definitely, it seems to me that nothing should be done to alter the mellowness of the logs themselves. The above mentioned method of treating the logs with three coats of oil gives the effect of being mellowed by age without giving opportunity for the disintegrating appearance that the actual weathering of the wood ofttimes suggests. This mellow beauty, however, may be emphasized more clearly by the slight contrast of a little color on the frames of door and sash and the doors and windows themselves.

Floors.

In general, the floors should be stained somewhat darker than the woodwork. Although the natural wood oiled is a thing of beauty in a floor, it is not practical because it shows every mark and soils quickly. If a floor is stained some soft shade of tobacco brown, the marking on its surface are less perceptible and the upkeep of it a matter of less time and trouble.

We prefer the floors to be fairly dark for reasons given before. Either pine or hardwood takes a tobacco brown stain very well—the chief difference is that the stain should be allowed to rest a little longer on the hardwood before wiping off the surplus.

If you wish a well-tested recipe for the stain, here it is:

In one and one-half gallons of turpentine, dissolve and mix well the following pigment colors ground in oil: five pounds of raw umber, two and a half pounds of yellow ochre, two pounds of chrome yellow (dark), one and one-half pounds of burnt sienna. After this is thoroughly stirred and mixed in the turpentine, add one gallon of boiled linseed oil. This, when thoroughly blended together gives you a rich brown stain for the floors that may be diluted for other woodwork if you choose.

It is to be applied to the floors with a brush rather generously—taking a section across the floor about as far as you can reach without getting into the mess. Go right across the room with your generous, even applications. Then back to the point of beginning, armed with a soft cloth, wipe off all surplus stain, so that the beauty of the grain of the wood shows through the particular color tone you have selected. Then take your next section of floor in the same way, being very careful not to lap your stain, thus producing a dark streak where the sections meet. The shade of your floor is regulated by the time the stain is left on, that is, the interval between brushing it in and wiping it off.

Possibly you will be satisfied with a floor that in time shows wear through your stain, as this very effect of worn boards is not undesirable when one is seeking a return to the primitive. In this case, the stain alone is sufficient for a year or so and then it should be retouched in worn spots here and there.

If, however, you wish to preserved the looks of your floor, you will apply two or three coats of floor varnish. This will increase the cost of your floor in the beginning, but it preserves both the color and the wood. The final coat of varnish gives a high gloss that is rather too garish to the artistic sense, but this may be toned down by a slight rubbing of the floor with fine steel wool which is better than sand-paper and more easily handled. This merely dulls down the varnish. (A "flat" varnish does not wear well on the floor.) Always remember to rub lengthwise with the boards, never with circular or cross-grain motion.

Have plenty of cloths at hand before you begin. Here is an excellent opportunity to get rid of all your old shirts and underwear, but be sure to take off the buttons first. Above all things, remember that when one of these cloths has been used to the saturation point it should be burned at once in a safe place, as there is nothing that has a greater tendency toward spontaneous combustion than these oil-soaked rags which have been used with friction. I have known such a cloth, carelessly left in a wad, to burst into flames in less than four hours.

A Suggested Color Scheme.

A soft tobacco brown stain may be used on the window- and door-frames and wiped off pretty vigorously, so that it is a little lighter than the floor. This brown is also applied to the door- and drawer-frames of cupboards, wardrobes and that sort of thing. A very little of this same stain may be put into the first coat of oil which is applied to the log work inside of the building to give a rich effect in a very light tone of wood-brown. In fact, this brown stain is your "stock." It may be thinned down to give any tone that you wish. Have some fun with it and work out effects for yourself.

Now, as to doors of all kinds, window sash and front of drawers in this suggested color scheme. There is a ready mixed forest green oil stain that looks almost green-black in the can—a very heavy color. To achieve the light apple green tone that is desirable, this may be reduced by mixing boiled linseed oil and turpentine half and half and blending this green stain with it in a ten to fifteen per cent proportion. This stain is then applied lightly with the brush and not wiped off. On white pine boards this will bring out all the color variants—knots and so-called defects in the wood—giving a gorgeous and variegated effect. (This was my reason for specifying lumber for the doors with as many "sound" knots as possible.) In general, fir, Norway pine, and some other woods of strong grain are too definitely fixed in a color of their own for this light green stain to cover it. The effect, however, which the stain brings about in this sort of wood is very lovely, but it is not so green. This light green stain if not given some surface treatment will turn into various blues and greens and fade out in time.

If you have elected to apply a light stain to your log walls, you will use a heavier tone of the stain on your ridge and purlins to emphasize them—but not so heavy as the floor stain, of course. The tones of your color should have the same sort of rhythm that is achieved in music by a stronger beat. To stain the rafters in a brown tone gives too heavy a ceiling, but if you want to play about with color, a pleasing effect may be had by mixing a stain from turpentine and oil and chrome yellow (dark). This gives a golden orange effect that makes a lovely contrast to your browns and greens.

In some particular room a color scheme may be carried out, even if you do not wish to do it throughout your building. A silver gray color—or weathered effect—for the under side of your roof boards, or ceiling, is obtained by applying a ready-mixed silver gray water-stain diluted to your taste. Practice with it on some small pieces of board first. One of Nature's own sky effects, that of gray distance as one looks up, is particularly effective in high-roofed rooms and is achieved by diluting this stain two to one.

Remember that any water stain, when first applied, looks very different from the way it appears when dry, so that your final decision must wait upon the drying out of your samples.

The above scheme of browns and greens and a silver gray ceiling with orange on the rafters is only one of a number of combinations, of course, that may be used. A cabin in varying tones of brown, for instance, is most attractive. Your floors may be blue and your ceilings red, if you are that kind of person. But have regard to harmony. This can be achieved even with the most garish combinations. Witness the sunset hues—the blending of colors in the rainbow—but it takes a masterhand to do it. The point is to select what suits you best—what you want to live with during your vacation. However, for the sake of the beauty of the grain of your wood, use stain rather than paint.

"Is there no place for paint in a cabin?" you demand with a show of reason.

Oh my, yes! One may have a heap of fun with paint if he has learned a certain amount of restraint. Right along with one instance of the use of this color scheme given above, paint was used in a way which surprised and delighted the beholder. Somewhere or other in your building you are going to have some projecting log-ends—out from an interior balcony or some such place. Carve out a head of a grotesque sort and paint it with brilliant colors to emphasize its features. Or roughly model the stair balusters, or turn a pillar into a totem pole in imitation of the Alaskan Indian effect. Or—there will be wasted log ends about, which may be turned over the the members of your crew to play with in off hours. Tell 'em that the best modeled head of the most ingenious design will be mounted in the cabin with the designer's initials inset as a perpetual memorial to his originality. You are likely to be amazed at the results of the work of some of them. Unsuspected ability along artistic lines will be brought to light. Probably the real artist will be found in the quiet chap whose silence you mistook for "dumbness"—or in the exasperating "kid" who is always playing at his work. Anyhow—the experiment has often been proved to be worth while.

Of Varnish Treatment.

Because the colors of your stain will fade out in time if not covered, it is wise to have some sort of a surface coating for their protection. To-day, as in the days of our ancestors, a very soft effect may be obtained by waxing everything. But in a log cabin, a well-rubbed varnish finish requires far less up-keep, is better for wear—and you don't care to go skating about a floor in your outing shoes, do you? This is a matter of personal taste, and many are all for waxed woodwork throughout. Don't forget, however, if choosing it, that a wax finish is difficult for amateurs to apply. Again, to keep it looking well takes a great deal of time away from fishing. To my personal notion, it has a much more sophisticated look than well-rubbed varnish.

Of course, a gloss finish may seem too bizarre to some, but on top of the green stain one may apply two coats of varnish, leaving plenty of time for the first coat to dry before applying the second. (Because of its better wearing quality, we use a floor varnish on all woodwork.) After applying the body varnish there are two or three ways of achieving a dull finish.

When both coats of varnish are dry, two coats of a "flat" varnish are applied to all woodwork except the floor. This produces about the same satiny finish or semi-gloss that is found on the trice-oiled logs. Another method is to rub the varnished woodwork lightly with a fine steel wool such as used in polishing up the kitchen aluminum.

The reason for not using varnish on the logs is that it gives an undesirable gloss to them. Moreover, the oil soaks into wood and is a better preservative—at a very much less cost.

Never forget that when applying one coat over another, sufficient time must elapse between coats for the under coat to dry out. Again, any finish such as oil or varnish applied over the water stain affects the color. The best way to treat the silver gray stain is to leave it alone.

Hunting and Fishing Lodge in New Brunswick.

CHAPTER FIFTEEN

THE SOPHISTICATED CABIN

Hitherto we have considered only the small cabin. The possibilities of size and complication, however, are almost unlimited. Go as far as you like if timber is available, freighting facilities at hand, and you can foot the bills for labor.

"Croixsyde" is complete.

In larger buildings requiring a great deal of log material I have found it feasible to ship Western red cedar even a thousand miles to the job. In one large cabin which had the complete equipment of a town house, the

What Aldrich calls a sophisticated cabin is what we'd now call standard. Aldrich's comments on heat, plumbing, and other utilities will strike you as quaint but troubling if you ponder the quality of the septic systems of his time. Nowadays you need more precise instructions for utilities, but Aldrich's recommendations are helpful for what they disclose of past practices.

Aldrich shows a cabin, with his trademark casement windows and dark rafters and purlins, featuring a small airtight stove and bunk beds. The stove would no longer be approved by your insurance company, and the bunks would not find approval from most adults. For children or grandchildren, however, these small bunk beds would allow you to keep some of the original rustic character. For guests, you might prefer to leave the cabin as is, a physical connection with the past, especially if you don't want visitors underfoot all summer.

Some cabins, though, are charming despite their flaws. I enjoy visiting a friend's frame-over-log cabin in which a ship's toilet was installed in a former firewood room off the back entrance. The room was in precarious shape a generation or two ago, and it hasn't improved since. The floor reminds me of a ski jump. The bottom of the door has been cut down repeatedly as the building has settled. To flush the finicky toilet requires hands, feet, and an engineering degree. The whole bathroom is a crazy mix of fixtures, found items, and oddments thrown together, but I gladly return to that friend's cabin. So, resign yourself to frequent summer visitors even if the structure is ramshackle quaint.

In modernizing an old cabin while retaining some of its original history or character, I stay within bounds set by the owners and by the cabin itself. Whatever the style, however, I encourage owners to include at least one gaslight that illuminates the kitchen and one other room, as insurance against a power failure in a storm. A gaslight provides safe, dependable, and convenient light, with an ample tank of liquefied petroleum gas. A kerosene lamp, such as an Aladdin lamp, gives comparable light, but, like other liquid-fueled lamps, it requires fresh fuel for the best operation. Kerosene, kept on hand for emergencies, deteriorates with age, leaving a gummy residue on wicks and lamp parts. And you have to trim and regulate a kerosene lamp carefully. Left unwatched, a kerosene lamp can turn into a combination torch and flamethrower.

Of course, a liquified-petroleum gaslight is not entirely problem-free. You have to keep a supply of mantles. A single moth can tear the fragile mantle. The other bugaboo of a gaslight is the spider. A spider web in the burner tube obstructs the gas and air flow, so the flame is sooty, and black patches of carbon form on the mantle. You can burn off the carbon and reuse the mantle sometimes, but heavily sooted mantles are usually hopeless. To get the web out, insert a wire through the tube and twirl the wire between your fingers to snag the web. When you remove the burner arm and tube, be careful not to disturb the air-volume slits at the base of the tube. An altered air volume can result in a balky, dirty-burning light.

A pressurized gasoline lantern is also excellent in an emergency. Indeed, this kind of lantern was common in cabins before rural electricity was widespread. Keeping gasoline indoors, however, is a risk many insurance companies urge you to avoid. Fill and light all such lanterns outdoors in a place where a fire could be contained. As with a kerosene lamp, familiarity leads to safer operation.

Few things can add or detract more than the lighting in a cabin. Most inappropriate light fixtures are easy to replace, but sometimes you have to search long and hard to find suitable lighting. In general, I avoid ceiling fixtures in favor of wall lights, table lamps, and inconspicuous accent lights. It's pleasant to shut off the electric lights and spend an evening under the glow of candles, gas, or kerosene. It's a form of time travel, as you imagine evenings when tired rural folk gathered around the kitchen table to talk in the circle of light before padding off to bed. When you

cost of this cedar plus the freight was only ten per cent of the cost of the building. The smaller and less complicated the building, however, the greater the proportionate cost of this long distance material delivered to the site—so this instance really means nothing to the small cabin builder. One merely remarks in passing that anything may be had if that is the sort of cabin you wish: hot and cold water, shower bath, even a lawn hose in your water supply. You may have an English basement kitchen equipped with dumb waiters. There may be laundry chutes and electric contrivances, as you desire.

The accommodations of your cabin may be increased by an increase of rooms within your building or by a multiplication of unit cabins, either attached or separate. This latter plan is often followed in tourist hotels or in large summer camps, and some more or less private residences make use of the same scheme. Then there may be a compromise between these two in the form of a central building designed with wings raying out from a lobby or loggia. All these designs, however, necessitate the services of architects and engineers to plan, design, and construct. Hence they are really outside of the scope of this book which is designed primarily to aid the man who is planning and building for himself.

Simplest way of increasing sleeping accommodations.

The simplest way for the latter to increase the sleeping accommodations of his cabin without stretching his building or adding more thereto, is by building double-deck bunks. There are several ways of working out this scheme. They may be built like an old-time four-poster in which the canopy top is in reality the upper bunk. Then there is the Pullman car idea—in which either the upper or lower bunk, or both, may be folded up against the wall out of the way during the daytime. Worst of all from the artistic viewpoint, but easiest to achieve, is the metal double bunk which is obtainable on the market.

Water Supply.

If you are going in for the primitive, your water supply will be carried in pails from a spring or stream of cold water perhaps a quarter of a mile away. (At least, part of it will be so carried in a pail; the remainder will sop the trail on each side for a quarter of a mile.) Then, most picturesque of all methods of obtaining water is the uncovered well decorated by an old-time well-sweep. Although most beautiful in effect upon the landscape, this water supply has its disadvantages, since many of these artistic old-time wells contained the body of an unbalanced stray cat or an unfortunate rabbit. To our modern sanitary notions this is not all it should be. So much for the primitive.

Running water may be piped without a great deal of intricate planning from any stream reasonably adjacent to your cabin. If this stream flows by at some point higher than the cabin, a small dam may be put in it to form a pocket—or a barrel may be sunk in it. This is then tapped and piped into the cabin, thus giving you a satisfactory and very inexpensive water supply. If you have such an arrangement as this, you can connect the piping with the water front of the kitchen stove and have hot and cold water without great expenditure for plumbing.

If, on the other hand, the water supply is below the cabin level—such as a lake or low-lying stream—a suction sieve and pump can be utilized, provided the difference in level is less than twenty feet. (The limit of "lift" for almost any valve is twenty feet.) The sieve is inserted in the lake or stream, and the pump—a small horizontal affair bolted to the floor with an upright handle conveniently placed for moving back and forth by hand—is located on the back porch or in come convenient spot within the cabin. This pump will force the water into an overhead tank near the cabin—a barrel or metal tank as you wish—and gravity will do the rest.

watch a person walk through a dark house with a kerosene lamp, you understand how easily people saw spirits and specters flickering through an old house.

Part of a cabin's charm is its ability to remove us from the pressures and devices of the modern world. By maintaining direct functional links with the past, we are reminded of alternative routes, of what we've lost and what we've gained. The intimate interior of a cabin should reflect something of the present and past owners, as well as something of the interplay between practical reality and recreational fantasy. The furnishing and lighting of your cabin should create an environment that gives pleasure to the emotions and the intellect, expressing your personal view of what is important and essential in life.

A pump similar to that described above may be used to force the water into a compression tank. This type of pump is so built that it forces also a small proportion of air along with the water, and this forms the pressure to send your supply where you wish. It can be so regulated that water may be piped to almost any reasonable distance from this tank. Consequently, if your water source is far away from your cabin, and at a greater depth than twenty feet below the cabin level, the pump and tank may be placed near the original supply to force the water anywhere needed.

If you have a stream or spring, it is possible to harness it with a pump known as a "hydraulic ram," which works automatically the year round, seldom needing to be adjusted. At some convenient point in the stream, or at your spring, a regulation sized barrel or small tank of barrel size should be sunk to form a head of water, and at a selected distance down the stream from the tank (but necessarily from four to six feet lower in elevation) this automatic pump or ram is placed and connected by galvanized piping. From this ram, water may be piped to almost any distance and to any reasonable height. I know of instances where the water supply has been thus forced a distance of fifteen hundred feet to a tank located in the hills more than one hundred and fifty feet above the stream. One particular ram has been in operation for many years without taking a vacation. Even in a Minnesota winter at thirty degrees below zero the music of the ram was heard issuing from a glorious cathedral of ice. This may give you some notion of the possibilities of harnessing a flowing stream with a ram which has the additional advantage of being reasonably inexpensive.

Then, of course, there are on the market various types of gasoline engines and pumps whereby the water supply can be taken from a lake—if that is a source you depend upon. Again—if you are building anywhere near a point where an electric line may be tapped, a still better arrangement of electric motor and pump may be installed for your service.

With any of these appliances, one may have in his cabin—large or small—a fully equipped bathroom, lavatories in the bedrooms and even hot water from the water front of your stove or from some type of separate heater. If you have no running or "live" water supply, the pump and tank system may be applied to a well.

It is best in all this plumbing arrangement, of course, to conceal the pipes as far as possible, both for the sake of protection from cold weather and also to hide your unsportsmanlike concession to civilization. This may be done by cutting channels for the pipes in the log walls and then boxing them or casing them in with boards. These casing boards should be screwed together so that they may be more readily taken apart if it ever becomes necessary to repair the plumbing. Of course, it is advisable to test all piping with an air-pump before closing in.

Keep in mind the fact that the whole system of piping must be so arranged with valves that it may be opened up and drained when you leave, so that water will not remain to freeze and burst your pipe while you are spending a peaceful winter in town. Again—don't forget to open and drain the traps of the sink, lavatories and closets for the same reason.

Waste Water and Sewage.

The carrying off and sanitary disposal of waste water and sewage is a most necessary matter. This can be taken away from the building into a series of two or more septic tanks. These may be the round steel tanks to be had on the market, shipped in to the job, or tanks built of concrete. The steel tanks are about four feet in diameter and four feet high and are buried in the ground. To install these you will, of course, need a plumber. In event of your electing the concrete tank, it will be well to get the drawings and diagram for it from some plumbing supply house or from your cement manufacturer. With this first aid equipment, concrete tanks have been built by inexperienced hands. They are often found on farms and in out-of-the-way places.

Now, from any type of tank there is a final overflow which should, if possible, be taken off into loose soil or a sand and gravel bed where it will seep away and thereby become purified before it reaches any stream or lake. (Although it is claimed by engineers that the overflow from the second tank is not in any way injurious.) These tanks, of course, should be located from fifty to one hundred feet away from the cabin—their placing depending on the contour of the land. A somewhat better method of disposing of the overflow, and one which avoids flies, is to pipe the waste water to an underground or "dry well." This is merely a good sized hole dug in the ground down to sand and gravel and protected by a wall of loose rock or brick laid up in bee-hive shape and covered with earth. If you are going in for any extensive scheme of sewage disposal, the assistance of a plumber who knows his business is extremely advisable.

It is possible to dispose of waste water from kitchen sink, bath tub, and lavatories separately. This may safely be piped into a well-removed spot for surface disposal in loose soil—or into the afore-mentioned "dry well"—and the actual sewage disposed of by the septic tank system.

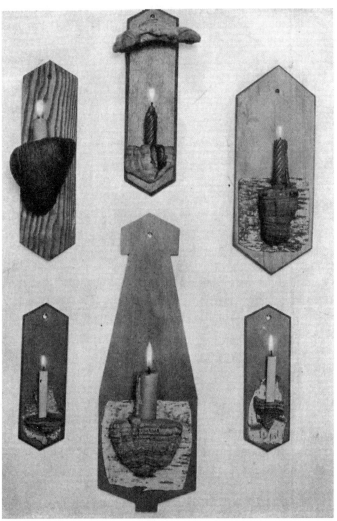

"It gives a lovely light."

Lighting Systems.

First of all, your candles are going to have a real use, aren't they, as well as a decorative effect? A log cabin is the place par excellence to discover how far a good deed shineth in this naughty world—provided you are old-fashioned enough to think Shakespeare is as good reading as Eugene O'Neill.

Anyhow—you are going to make some use of candles, and so let them be "dipped tapers" in appearance whether actually dipped by hand or by some of Rockefeller's machinery. Long slim tapers will wave tiny yellow handkerchiefs at you in friendly fashion as you sit at your rustic board—or light the way to bed for your guest. At least let them have such blithe part as this in your abode of the primitive. For—as Edna St. Vincent Millay hath it, "They give a lovely light." There isn't a chance that you haven't learned that delicious bit, is there?

> "My candle burns at both ends;
> It will not last the night;
> But, ah, my foes, and oh, my friends—
> It gives a lovely light!"

In a rushy world, what could be a more alluring or more sinister word than that?

The next step away from the primitive is the kerosene lamp which proves very satisfactory in cabins which do not indulge in a lighting system. If you are able to obtain a high grade kerosene, you will find on the market a lamp designed like the old ship lamp, which meets your requirements and fits in with the general idea of the building. It gives a good light, and is appropriate in its simplicity. It may be had in the bracket lamp form with single burner or in the more popular swinging lamp variety with two, three or four burners. They are particularly successful when used with a high grade kerosene. Then there are various types of kerosene and gasoline burning mantel lamps and lanterns.

Of course, if you are near an electric line that may be tapped, light may be brought into your cabin by the simple method of knob and tube wiring. But keep well in mind that exposed wires in a cabin do not add to the effect of rustic simplicity.

If you are going in for a more or less pretentious forest lodge, you will probably have your private electric plant. There are many types of these on the market, run by gasoline engines, with the generator either attached directly to the engine shaft or separate. These outfits may be obtained either with or without a series of storage battery cells. Such a plant will supply electricity for all purposes around the place. Obviously, you will want your generating plant in a separate building—or at least with its own private room in your boat-house.

In selecting your type of plant, make up your mind how much work it is expected to do. They may be had from various manufacturers ranging from the small plant which supplies a few lights up to one which would answer the requirements of a popular summer resort.

Now, as to wiring. As overhead wires extending from your plant to your building along series of poles are more or less unsightly, it is advisable to spend a very little more money on lead cable to carry them underground. The cost of a cable for a large cabin I recently completed, supplying about two hundred lamps, as well as various pumps and every conceivable type of kitchen equipment, proved to be less than fifteen percent greater than an overhead line—considering the necessary expenditure in the upkeep of the latter. It certainly more than made up for its extra cost in the appearance of the grounds. A great advantage of the underground cable lies in the fact that it is impervious to water and may be carried through streams or laid on the bed of a pond.

To return to the matter of wiring the cabin itself. In order to have no exposed wires, one may use "BX," "Greenfield," and flexible conduit. Regular pipe conduit may be used, of course, in some places. Although this work is absolutely not for the amateur but for the accredited electrician, the method of utilizing these conduits so as to have all wires concealed may be one of several. Before the door frames are set, lines are carried up from the basement through the floor along a channel which has been chiseled into the log-ends that are afterward covered by the door frames. Lines are then run through the walls by boring holes through the logs and flexible conduits threaded through as each log is laid. Then where it is necessary to carry lines across horizontally, a channel is cut into the top of a log and the conduit strung along this channel before the log above is laid in position. In this manner, with careful forethought, concealed lines may be carried all over the building to outlets and switches. Naturally, this necessitates a complete lighting plan worked out before the building is begun.

In case of drop lights, the lines are carried in a similar way up through the walls and across the top of truss members or purlins and ridge log and dropped through for ceiling light.

Heating.

First of all—how are you planning to use your building? For late spring, summer, and early fall in the ordinary inhabited spaces of the temperate zone of North America—the fireplace and range will be sufficient for good scouts. If your wood supply is plentiful, you may have wood stoves.

If, however, you have planned to live in your cabin in cold weather, you have built a basement and have allowed in your chimney for a heating plant flue. Since cabins are usually built in the woods where this sort of fuel abounds, the best, most natural, and economical heating plant is a wood-burning, warm-air furnace of which there are many types. There are several pipeless furnaces on the market which supply heat for the building through one large central register in the floor. The return air—cold air from the floor—is taken down around the edges of this register, thus forming circulation.

If you wish a piped furnace, you have several choices of those which have a dome or hot air chamber on top from which the pipes lead off to the rooms you wish heated. In connection with this, a return pipe is taken down from the floor probably of the largest room to bring about proper circulation. A pipe through the basement wall taking in outside air is not absolutely necessary with this sort of furnace, but it gives an assurance of ventilation.

If your building is a two-story affair of the rambling type, you may still use a wood-burning warm-air system, but one assumes in this case that you have a generating plant and may utilize electricity to force the air through the pipes by a fan system. In this event, your heating engineer has laid out a plan of smaller piping which is obviously not only less expensive but less trouble to conceal. In the larger furnaces a horizontal firebox will take six or eight sticks of four-foot cord wood at one firing—or may be so built, if specified, that either wood or coal may be used.

In a Minnesota cabin of twelve rooms which my client wished equipped with a wood-burning furnace, winter weather at twenty below demanded about one and one-half cords of four-foot wood every week. In a more commodious building such as a hotel or lodge which takes care of guests who are always notoriously chilly when not raving over the heat, other and more "citified" heating facilities than the wood-burning furnance must be supplied. Steam or hot water is your choice then—heated by either oil or coal, depending on which market is the more convenient.

Whatever sort of furnace you order, give your dealer a set of plans so that he may figure the cubical contents to be heated, the glass area of your building—that sort of thing. Then he will ship you the furnace in sections ready to be set up—and probably satisfactory.

If you have a water supply, by all means have a coil put in your furnace and a galvanized iron hot-water tank either near the furnace or up in the kitchen. This tank may be hooked up also with the water-front in the kitchen range so that you may have hot water even in non-furnace weather. Or, of course, a small auxiliary heater may be connected with the water tank.

CHAPTER SIXTEEN

LOG CABIN FURNITURE

The man who builds a log cabin and then thinks his wilderness home is complete is the sort of person who would try to tell a joke and leave out the point. Having a non-leaky roof, reasonably plumb walls, and a fireplace which will draw, let us not therewith be content. These are merely a good start.

There is a great temptation to approach the discussion of log cabin furniture by a series of "don'ts." However, psycho-analysis warns us of the danger of inhibitions, so we shall let fly only one rather large and rather comprehensive "don't": "DON'T ship to your new cabin the junked contents of your attic and storeroom in town." You desire a wilderness home—a restful abode of the primitive—not an Asylum for the Aged and Infirm Furniture.

When we built our cabin on the North Shore of Lake Superior, there were many guesses among the curious natives as to what sort of furniture "city people" were going to have. Our neighbors—bless 'em—trekked in with their mail order catalogs of alluring bargains. When we thanked them but "regretted exceedingly," they began to have doubts of our financial standing. There was only one reason in the world, in their eyes, for not only eschewing knock-down catalog houses and ready-made millwork, but refusing to become interested in furniture that "you don't have to pay all down on right away."

There was one brass bed in the neighborhood, and natives flocked to see it. It had been bought by the careful savings of a lad who had worked at all sorts of odd jobs—hiding away his earnings where not even a bank could get hold of them—until he had enough for this investment. And it

Aldrich, like some other architects of his time, crafted the furnishings for each cabin. He warns against using furniture discarded from your winter home—advice that is usually ignored.

When my family vacationed on Lake Superior's north shore, we stayed in Hovland with an elderly Swedish musician named Werner, who rented a collection of cabins. He gave his resort the Swedish name Bel Mansro. Cabins were named, Nor Stuga (North Star) and Lil Stuga (Little Star), for example. Werner's personal cabin, the main lodge, wandered all over the countryside with additions. Aldrich would have shaken his head in dismay over the mistreated logs and the floors that undulated from room to room. When my parents first stayed with Werner in the 1930s, he charged one dollar per person per day, for room, board, a fishing boat, and a guide. Once the guests became familiar with the homey atmosphere, they would save articles to contribute to Werner's cabins, and every season saw a new influx of cast-off treasures.

Werner had a baby grand piano in the biggest room of the main lodge. Over the piano was draped a red cloth with long black fringe. My mother said it was a Spanish shawl someone had given to Werner. Bits of the shawl's fringe had been carried off to become mouse nest. The walls around the piano were covered by an assortment of moth-eaten animal hides and chipped porcelain plates. Floor lamps from grand old houses and wobbly bedside tables from averages homes were clustered on discarded carpets and rugs of every possible style, the way a troop of elderly prostitutes might gussy up a rural bordello. This wretched assemblage actually worked in Werner's setting, it was so flamboyantly garish. In a private cabin, however, similar collections appear tawdry.

You probably prefer a more unified effect in your cabin, with perhaps a few of those odd elements. It's charming when owners include pieces significant to them, giving the cabin a personal history drawn from their own past. I find it equally appropriate to retain something belonging to past owners, acknowledging the cabin's special place in the lives of many people.

Aldrich's way of personalizing a cabin was to make the furniture himself and encourage others to follow his example. At one time writers and outdoor advocates made much of their own furniture, benches and chairs and more ambitious pieces such as dressers and sideboards, often overlaid with natural materials like tree bark. This trend seems to have peaked some time ago. Aldrich's designs are more at home on a veranda than a room where comfort is desired. There's not much difference between plopping down on a log by a campfire and sitting on a handmade "rustic" chair on a porch. The furniture shown in the Wa-wa-tay Post, for example, looks neither comfortable nor stable.

With tables and chairs of birch logs, the bark continues to look presentable with the passing of the years. Birch, however, must be kept dry to prevent serious and rapid interior decay. Your cats will hardly be able to walk past a table or chair without swatting at dangling shreds of bark. Eventually they will remove all the loose bark, leaving only the hard polished bark.

Some antique shops have rustic pole or log furniture of good and tested design. Using the furniture outdoors makes it look drab from weathering. You can revive the finish by sanding, staining, and applying fresh varnish or even paint, although I recommend using paint only as a last resort. At Bel Mansro, Werner went hogwild and painted his log cabin in candy stripes: the logs in strong red and the chinking in wide white bands. Restful it was not. Paint on a log cabin is very difficult to undo. Werner's cabin deteriorated because the paint acted like bark, holding moisture in the wood. The logs looked solid, but a poke here or there revealed large areas of spongy rot under the paint. So if you wish to brighten up your log cabin, proceed with considerable caution and seek expert advice on the use of fungicide in the paint. Wood stains also

must be granted that it would be hard to find any article of furniture which has given its owner more pleasure than that extremely large, extremely shiny and extremely robust brass bed. Grief stalked at his heels when he heard it rumored that the city people would probably have a larger and shinier one. However, we soon put him at his ease by asking his help in scouring the woods for fit saplings for a four-poster.

Let us exclude at once the log cabin owner who has the taste and means to select his rustic furniture from some one of the many excellent handicraft shops where they really know how to design and build things sturdily fit. This chapter is intended to be helpful to him who prefers to do things with his own little hatchet.

Those who wish their wilderness home to evince a complete return to the primitive are likely to fall into one of three classes—ruling out the attic ransacker with his van load of inebriated tables, disgorging lounges, bamboo whatnots, and whining platform rockers.

First comes the crate, box and barrel-stave chap, although, as a matter of fact, there is a good geal of usable lumber in all of these. Chair seats and backs can be made of crate boards, a fairly comfortable chair out of a barrel cut down to fit the anatomy, and cupboards out of boxes—never forgetting to lay aside thin boards for drawers. However, the boys in the lumber camps call this style of doing things the "hay-wire-and-gunny-sack" method—and so, unless your artistic grasp and ability are confirmedly no more than this, work out of this class as rapidly as possible.

The board, slab, and edging workman is the second degree. He at least gets over to the nearest country sawmill—be it an established mill or one of the portable variety. He probably has more or less ability as a carpenter and joiner and achieves more artistic and comfortable effects from his material. His chair bears evidence of some idea in design—like the lazy-back chair illustrated—and his tables are of good proportions and are substantial.

Even though your furniture maker achieves the highest class, the third degree of artistry in his cabinet work—that of Brace and Bit and Native Timber creative genius, he is likely to depend for much of his material upon the aforementioned country sawmill.

Wa-wa-tay Post has hand-made furniture.

require care and testing. You can easily redo a chair but not a floor stain that looks ugly or wears badly under traffic.

Furniture Material

Of the native timber used by the amateur in making furniture, birch is the favorite because it is usually at hand and fits in well with almost any color scheme of building, but this is not the only wood which is effective. There is ironwood, poplar, hickory, cedar—any of these saplings to your liking. It is well to keep in mind when you mortise one piece of green sapling to another that there will, in time, be a shrinkage which will have to be taken care of. This is where the factory has the better of the amateur craftsman in wood. It uses only seasoned wood, and therefore the factory-made piece is less likely to become rickety in the course of a season or two. Herein is indicated an argument in favor of your planning next summer's work this year, and selecting your wood in order to let it have at least a year's drying out ready for your hand.

Very little further suggestion can be made as to the selection of the kind of timber for your furniture, as that will more or less be determined by the trees available. On our North Shore place we have the various pines and birches, and for our own cabin have chosen young birch of the pinkish gray or brown variety rather than the chalk white, as it seems to us warmer and more pleasing in lending itself to the coziness of the room. In the Studio Cabin, cedar with the bark on has proven its worth in various articles of furniture. A most beautiful effect has been gained by an extremely artistic neighbor of ours in the use of the silver gray driftwood in rare and grotesque formations; and there comes to memory a satisfyingly lovely table in the study of the late Enos Mills, the Colorado naturalist, formed of the weathered root of a gnarled and tortured old tree uprooted at timber line. The artist finds new things in old.

There is no limit to the number of pieces of furniture which can be formed out of the saplings native to your place if your patience and your lumber hold out.

Handmade chair -Squantum

Your fancy may range from the three- or four-legged stools to chairs of all sorts and descriptions—even a chaise longue and a pull-out settee-davenport; from the most ordinary table with a leg at each corner to refectory boards of intricate workmanship and great beauty of design; from the simplest shelves (that are at least straight enough to keep the dishes from sliding off) to the buffet at which you can point with pride. As to benches—with or without backs—racks or wood boxes, hat trees, washing-stands, four-poster beds, book shelves and fireside settles—these are cabin commonplaces which your wife will undoubtedly believe can be tossed off as a morning's work. At least that is my personal experience with wives.

Furniture details

The Tools.

Now, as for tools needed: A brace and bits or auger, chisels, plane, hammer and saw, and a good knife for whittling—these will take you far. Heavy casing nails for pinning the saplings after they are driven into the holes will be needed, and a screwdriver and screws of various lengths if board slats are to be utilized for the backs of chairs and benches. While it is possible to hew out and plane off directly from your own logs the planks for table tops and seats of chairs, you will save time and will probably achieve a better effect by using dressed boards from your sawmill. Very artistic tables whose "chassis" were made on the job had birch tops glued-up at the mill and shipped along with screens and sash.

Furniture Details.

The simplest articles of furniture and the most quickly made are stools, and these, though make-shiftish, may be wrought with a sufficient artistry to enable them to keep places near the hearth even after

more elaborate furniture is designed and worked out. A short section of log is split in two and hewn off smooth for the top side of the stool while the under or rounded side has holes bored in it slantwise so that the legs will splay, or straddle, when inserted. This can well become a unit design for a good-looking chair if the log chosen be sufficiently wide for two holes to be bored slantwise in the topside also for splayed uprights to be inserted. These form the solid vericals to which cross-pieces are attached, thus making a comfortable back for the tired vacationer. These pieces, by the way, may be scrolled instead of plain crossbars—in imitation of the ladder-back chairs of our great-grandmothers. A plank seat may be utilized in the same way instead of the log section. The pitch of the seat and the splay of the back are the secret of comfort in a camp-made chair.

In setting the legs in, make the holes an inch to an inch and a half in diameter. It is best to select a length of sapling of greater diameter than this and whittle the ends to drive into the hole. This makes also for stability. The lengths of these pieces are adjusted for height by your artistic sense unless you have measured drawings, and you may make more than one try at it before you are content. A stool is quainter if lower than a chair, and it is level on the topside.

A refectory bench is most easily built like an elongated stool—but as half a log is a bit unwieldy, if long, for moving about it is advisable to make your table bench of plank or boards. Select ten- to twelve-inch boards the length of the table, and under each end of one of these set

slantwise a section of board about eighteen inches long, in place of the set-in legs, using cleats under the bottom side of the bench. These small board sections on either end of the seat plank are adjusted to proper height by placing them six to eight inches from the ends of the seat and splaying them six to eight inches out. They are held rigid by two narrow boards attached to the sides of these uprights directly under the bench top or seat. These side and end pieces can be cut or scrolled into any artistic shape, curves and arches that fancy dictates. However, an inverted V, cut up into the standards to simulate tapering legs suffices for all but the most ambitious workman.

"TRAILSYDE"
·DINING·TABLE·
·CHAIRS·
·BENCH·

Furniture details.

In making a table, the purpose for which it is to be utilized will more or less determine its dimensions other than the standard height of thirty inches. A table-top three by eight feet will accommodate ten people, as the space conventionally allotted to the comfort of each ordinarily sized guest is two feet at the table. If you are making the whole thing yourself, cut the plank or boards for table-top according to determined length and fasten together on the underside by battens with screws from underneath. A strip of dressed board three inches wide as an apron or drop piece is then set from two to three inches in from the edge all around and screwed into cleats.

In selecting pieces for legs, try to secure straight saplings, fairly even of diameter, in right proportion to the table-top. A three by six foot table, comfortably seating eight people, will stand four sturdy legs up to five inches in diameter without clumsiness. When these are cut to the right length for height, bore a hole in each five to seven inches from the bottom and insert cross saplings for the ends about three inches in diameter. In these cross-pieces, about three to four inches each way from center points, bore another hole to insert two lengthwise pieces—preferably less in diameter. Atop these lengthwise pieces a board may be fastened, forming a useful lower shelf as well as aiding in stability. The upright legs and the pieces mortised together form, as a table chassis, a rigid framework which prevents the legs from spreading.

The upper end of each leg is then slightly squared to fit snugly inside the apron when the table-top is set on. The apron is firmly fastened to the legs by long screws.

Standard Heights

Some suggestions as to standard sizes and heights may be helpful.

The conventional height of the dining table is thirty inches and that of a dining chair—floor to seat—eighteen inches with an eighteen- to twenty-inch height of back. This chair should have a straight back and an almost level seat. In lieu of chairs, a refectory bench, either with or without a back, is found much more practical in a log cabin. If cushions are to be used on any chairs, the thickness of these should be allowed for in the eighteen-inch height. A generous-sized seat for an ordinary chair is about eighteen inches square—an armchair being somewhat wider than it is deep.

For greater comfort in lolling about, a chair should be made with a seat somewhat lower than this and pitched toward the back from one to two inches. The back of each chair is also proportionately inclined. Take note of a rocking chair if you are old-fashioned enough to have one about, and you will discern, when it is at rest, the angle of back and seat that makes for its comfort. Never construct a perfectly straight-backed chair unless you wish your visitors to take an early departure. To be sure, our Puritan ancestors had straight-backed chairs and sat in them—but they also had hair shirts and wore them.

Even rockers are not out of the question for the amateur builder if he wishes to try his hand at one. Let him secure from his hardware dealer in the city some two, three and four inch carriage bolts and go to it. These are found almost a necessity in fastening rockers firmly to the chair to make it stable. A bolt, too, has this advantage over a mortised piece—the bolt may be drawn up taut even though the wood is green.

Using the shaggy birch.

As to Designs.

The "Trailsyde" design of tables and benches and chairs is exceedingly simple, yet it is one that we do not tire of in the least. Birch columns fitted into horizontal pieces for a base—protected from scraping when moved about by a thin board planed for a "slip-easy" or "shoe," fastened on the under side.

From the simplest stool, and a hat-rack formed by inserting into a short length of log, a sapling with its branches stubbed into convenient lengths of hanging-hooks, it seems a far cry to the pull-out settee, yet the construction of the latter depends chiefly on the lesson of driving in the legs and spindles. The seat board is hinged and is folded when utilized as a settee and the seat is built low enough not to make a doubled pad or two thin single mattresses—one atop the other—too high for comfort in sitting. A sapling naturally curved is used for topping the spindles of back and arms—and the unevenness of the curve of it may even add to the artistic appearance of the finished article. It makes a most convenient "lounging around" place for the front of the fire, and is a welcome addition to any camp where an over-night visitor is likely to happen in and otherwise deprive some member of the household of a bed.

There is often a fancy for built-in settles or benches around an ingle nook. These are the most uncomfortable things to be found anywhere unless the seats are low—fourteen or fifteen inches from the floor—and pitched well back toward the wall. Give plenty of width to the seat— Twenty to twenty-four inches—so that there will be room to tuck a cushion behind you. The backs of these settles should be about three feet high from the seat and slanted three or four inches for comfort. Thus you have the old-time effect without its exceeding discomfort. Only such lovers as are pictured in the well-known "Home-keeping Hearts" were ever really unconscious of the stiffness of the primitive wooden bench.

Frames for bed springs and mattresses—which are among the few things to be brought from town—may be made similar to the table chassis—leaving the four corner posts long and rounding them off on the top or ornamenting them with the various tree fungi to be found in any woods. The common birch fungi, by the way, make very pleasing candle sconces. Various types of them are shown here.

Landscaping in General.

Personally, I think that to do landscaping about a forest home is rather an insult to nature, but I am aware that there are those who feel differently about the matter. I well recall visiting the log villa of a most important member of society and finding the latter strolling about his grounds ordering vistas cut in every direction. Trees that were more than twice his age were ruthlessly removed from the landscape by his henchmen. With a wave of his white ringed hand he announced patronizingly, "Nature has really done a great deal for this place." Indeed, Nature had—by making Lake Superior immovable and its rocky headlands difficult to blast away.

Probably as you built, you inadvertently destroyed some trees, so that it is the part of wisdom to reforest a bit and prepare for a green future. Coniferous trees which can be found back in the woods growing entirely too close together may be lifted carefully out of their native soil and transplanted in groups near your cabin. As we have inferred before, little trees are fond of each other's company. Moreover, grouping will enable one to protect them better until they are large enough to take care of themselves. The snowshoe rabbit has a penchant for small transplanted trees, particularly white pine and spruce. He has been known to eat cedars as well—two and three foot trees right down to the stub. (If you don't believe it, I'll show you the stubs.) So if you are going to transplant trees in a rabbit infested country, it is wise to encircle each group of little transplants with chicken wire until they are large enough to fight rabbits.

Bushes may be transplanted into lovely groupings and in the course of a year or so a wonderful wild flower garden may be developed by a selective transplanting or careful gathering of choice seeds.

Terraces out in your grounds may be anything from a few flat stones for your chair to rest upon to a more or less artificial effect of stone pillars or rough modeled log posts carrying log railings about a flat stone floor.

Garden Furniture.

The simplest garden furniture is made by driving four sticks in the ground, connecting them with cross-pieces and laying a couple of planks upon them. From this, as his practice piece, the amateur furniture maker may develop all sorts of things: Rustic benches and tables, gateways and archways, pergolas, trellises for vines—anything that may be fitted into the landscape without actually affronting it. Don't overdo the matter, however. When your garden furniture begins to call attention to itself rather than to emphasize the loveliness of nature, tear out that last thing you put in. Remember that the Creator himself stopped at the end of each day's work to make sure that it was good and enough of its kind.

In urging you to discover talent within your hand and brain for the furniture craft, there is no desire to gainsay the fact that your finished product is not going to look like the drawing-room furniture of a villa on Long Island. No matter how clever you may be revealed, prepare yourself for a result that is crude and bearing the imprint of the amateur at log cabinet-work. Don't try to conceal this. Brag about it. Point to it with pride. It is the very mark that in an antique shop brings a large bonus. It is moreover, the one thing that gives it value—this expression of your own individuality in the joyous achievement of what fulfils your primitive needs.

No need to emphasize the fun you are going to have working out your ideas, as glory of achievement surpasses all other human delights.

"Squantum" shows artistic use of driftwood.

CHAPTER SEVENTEEN

THE CONCLUSION OF THE WHOLE MATTER

There is no real end to a book on cabin building. First of all because the art itself is only just now opening its sleepy eyes to its own place in the world. Then—if one's cabin has been a growth of his own, he will find that it is never completed. Perfection in anything, for the best of us, is a long way off. There will always be tinkering to do—inside of the cabin and out. Perchance the last attempt one made at a thing of beauty has been a grotesque failure. Tear it out and never regard it as Love's labor lost. Love's labor is never lost. All experience becomes valuable to the man whose heart is in the work of his head and hands.

You will find that each bit you do widens and deepens your love for your forest home. However conventional and standardized your abode in the city must needs be, let your dwelling of peace in the heart of the woods be a true expression of the greater personality that hides within you. You will discover a lot of things—interesting things—about yourself as you build your dream home. Let each bit of handiwork upon it be a veritable part of the Real You manifested outwardly, unashamedly to the world.

After all, what can a book of this sort be but a "patteran"—or, as the dictionary most unprofessionally hath it, "patrin" for other Gypsies to follow?

As the African savage dons the high hat and stiff bosom shirt of evening wear as a sign of his conversion to Christianity, and Lo, the poor Indian, demands the most sophisticated of canned goods as his government rations, even so the descendants of generations of high-hatted Puritan forebears don flannel shirt and khaki trousers as a sign of their

Aldrich ends his book on a philosophical chord, perhaps a bit high-flown. Although such concerns are not related directly to the practical issues of design or construction, knowing the attitudes of those who came before helps us understand the works they left behind. Old cabins are more alive and intimate when we have glimpses of those who first dreamed them and then brought the dream into reality.

Some of Aldrich's expressions and ideals seem outdated and irrelevant now. Keep in mind, however, that The Real Log Cabin, *in print for almost two decades, was a source of information and inspiration for many cabin owners and armchair dreamers. From its first printing in 1928 until Aldrich's death almost twenty years later,* The Real Log Cabin *represented a long-standing aspect of the American psyche in the form of pioneering do-it-yourself-ism. Similar attitudes have survived, although the style and speed of cabin building became wide open in the boom years after the Second World War. In that prosperity many ordinary folk began to carve out their versions of the Aldrich dream, a significant departure from Aldrich's heyday, when few but the rather well-to-do could afford the rustic leisure of a handcrafted cabin in the woods. Many northern lakes were staked out by retired tycoons who sat in splendid log cabins built to their exact wishes. I need hardly stress, of course, the irony of affluent business people attempting to achieve the simple pleasures of life in a log cabin tucked away on a rustic shore.*

I have left The Real Log Cabin *intact as much as possible. To understand the evolution of summer cabins into summer homes, we should go*

back to the beginning of the process and to the attitudes of the early days of the recreational cabin. In retaining the book's warts, blemishes, and embarrassing comments, I trust that today's reader will be able to separate the wheat from the chaff and will be aware of how attitudes subtly color and focus the ways we structure our leisure worlds. That Aldrich viewed his cabins from a man's point of view, for example, is historic fact, in keeping with his era. Knowing that today's standards for cabins are broader, we have to decide what to keep from the past and what to eliminate or replace.

Although I'm inclined to leave well enough alone, in my commentary I've tried to point out the plus and minus features, especially for cabins built before the shift toward second homes. If you plan to conserve or remodel your cabin, I hope this book will help in retaining and enhancing the historic elements that give charm and character to a building, while updating your cabin to a standard suitable for today.

Since there has been something of a boom in log cabins recently, I have written some additional chapters about alternative styles of log treatment. You may discover well-developed local traditions for handling logs, besides the ways I've described here. I hope that somewhere in these pages you'll find a design or style that suits your needs in the intimate task of crafting your cabin to echo the past while facing the future.

conversion to the Gospel of the Out-of-Doors, and their children become Boy Scouts and Campfire Girls with inhibitions for any but plainest fare.

There is no bluff about the keen pursuit of out-of-door joys on the part of the much maligned youth of the present day. What if they are restive under restraint? They bow meekly enough to the rules of sportsmanship. Much of this very restiveness is understandable, too, for there are so many unjustified "verbotens" imposed by life in the city.

Aside from the fine organizations of Scout and Campfire which stress the teachings of all-around woodscraftmanship and forthright sturdiness of character—often with picturesque symbols of Indian lore and tradition—there are numberless summer camps (all-year-round camps for that matter) for our boys and girls. You have seen their eyes sparkle and their faces flush even when they are talking about "camp," haven't you? "Sana mens in corpore sano."

Nowhere else can emphasis be laid with such telling effect upon the Beautiful and Good of the old Greeks as in the Cathedral of the Forest. It is a mighty poor specimen of young folk that does not show a quick response to the Ideal when set before them in an environment of natural beauty.

There is little question but that a man who loves the Out-of-Doors and prides himself upon having the characteristics of a "square shooter" and a "dependable scout" makes the most successful business man as well as the best friend. There is a proud boast among the sportsmen of this country that no recognized and honest-to-goodness out-of-doors man has ever been found guilty of a major offense against society. Once upon a time it was thought that an exception to this rule had been discovered, but it came to light later that the criminal had merely been a cross-country automobilist who stopped at trout streams along his route and took out under-sized fish.

Ever since the time when twelve men—all but the traitor among them being out-of-door men and most of them fishermen—were chosen to carry through the greatest conservation project ever put forth, it has seemed that the real thinkers and real achievers of the world have been those who refused to focus their eyes upon the pettiness at hand and turned them to look into the great spaces.

CHAPTER EIGHTEEN

SQUANTUM

The cabin Squantum was designed and partly built by Maurice Maine, a Minneapolis architect and associate of Aldrich. Aldrich built the fireplace system but may not have helped with the log work. Squantum is in the stockade style, with short logs that are easier to handle, so Maine may have worked alone, calling in extra hands only for the ridge and purlins. Although Squantum and Aldrich's Trailsyde are adjacent and were built at roughly the same time, there are many differences. Aldrich promoted a conventional rustic style, simple and straightforward. Maine created an artistic experience, with abundant and precise detail at virtually every stage of construction and finishing. Whereas as Aldrich cabin inspires a homey feeling of rural life, a Maine cabin is full of idiosyncratic delights and personal touches.

The simple breakfast nook in Squantum, for example, faces a tiny elevated fireplace with strands of golden straw carefully revealed in the mortar. On the wall around the fireplace, Maine laid out a scroll pattern of carved and stained wood. He never completed it, although he rendered the whole in wonderful sketches and a full-size template executed in Minneapolis. Also in the breakfast nook, a little man carved from driftwood wears a beaded grass skirt and holds up one end of the table. The log walls of the nook were shaved, smoothed, and worked with a circular gouge to add texture and vertical line to the logs, which were then treated with a pale blue opaque stain. This tiny room, with its plain board ceiling and carefully worked walls, is very successful.

Maine personalized so much of his cabin that it's difficult to describe. He carved and hand-colored the door handles and cupboard latches. On the end of each beam that jutted into the interior, he carved a fanciful creature, skillfully

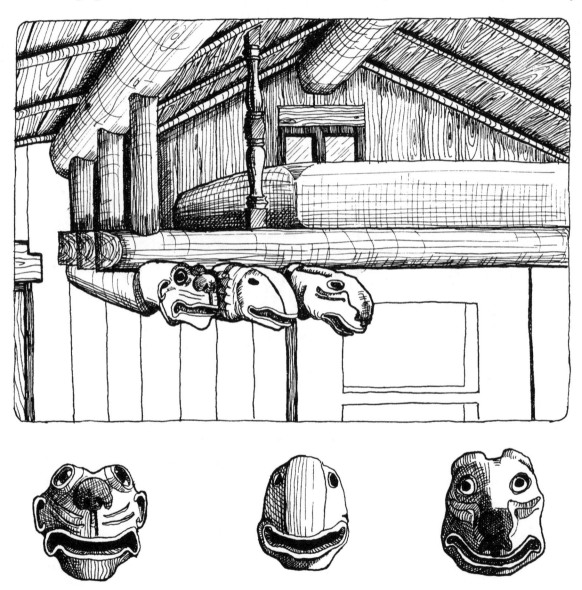

executed and delicately colored. Each carving was given a name and was described fully in a handmade book that was left in the cabin, Ye Tales of Squantum. When I first set foot in Squantum many years ago, I was overwhelmed by the precise intricacy, as if I'd slipped back in time into a dreamworld of people now departed.

As delightful as it is, however, Squantum shares problems with more common buildings. Like Aldrich, Maine built too close to the ground. Maine made portions of his roof flatter than even Aldrich would have dared. Maine's roof problem is not quite so pronounced, though, because the cabin is small, making the span short. The low roof is properly built, but it is a limiting factor. Indeed, I think Maine abandoned his plan for a bedroom, expanded kitchen, and bathroom because the roofline was too low for an eave-sided addition. The cabin, loaded with special features and built with dollhouse precision, is very small, with only a modest kitchen, the breakfast nook, and then one main room where the bed, furniture, and fireplace compete for space.

How should Squantum be treated today? It's too small for a typical family, but it's too unique to subject to a quick-fix addition. The present owners live nearby and have saved Squantum for special evenings and occasional overnights. To update or expand Squantum in keeping with its original design would require much planning and an ample budget. The most extreme alternative would be to build an entirely new summer home that encapsulated the main room of the old cabin as a unique den or living room. That option would radically change Squantum's look and feel but would protect the old logs from decay, while keeping the interior intact for everyday use and enjoyment of the classic craftsmanship and special style of this work of art.

Breakfast nook.

CHAPTER NINETEEN

POST AND SILL

Post-and-sill construction is commonly credited to French fur traders, who introduced the style wherever they explored and settled. Much of that contribution was lost when the English ousted the French and treated their achievements as minor, in the way that historic records tend to emphasize the images and prejudices of the winners. For this reason, possibly, Aldrich was unaware of post-and-sill construction. He thought the simpler pioneer use of round logs was the first style of construction by white American settlers. Their earliest buildings, however, were in European styles adapted to native materials and smaller, less experienced work forces. The English houses were timbered buildings similar to those in England and on the Continent. The remaining French settlers continued using the post-and-sill technique, with steeply pitched roofs to shed water.

The post-and-sill technique is practical and efficient. A great deal of carpentry is involved in creating hewn stock, grooves and tongues, mortise and tenon joints, locking lap joints and pegged splices, but the task is fairly straightforwaard. A small force can erect a large structure because the wall logs are seldom long or unwieldy. Towering lock-pin rafters, of course, require considerable skill and teamwork to raise into place, but they are conveniently fitted on the ground. This kind of construction lends itself to prefabrication, preparing major parts in advance. The fur-trade journals reveal that French traders often pulled apart their old post-and-sill buildings to reuse the sound logs in new buildings.

All the vertical logs are joined to sills and plates with mortise and tenon joints, and all the verticals are grooved to hold the wide tongues of the horizontal logs in place. Additional verticals frame openings. Doors have full-length verticals at each side. A small window is likely to have a full-length vertical on one side and on the other side a short vertical to describe the height of the window. The building is largely a repetition of standard elements, the same for both small and large structures. The process is self-evident, although there are tricks you learn only by tackling the job.

Some years ago a friend of mine who worked at a Boy Scout camp was looking for a way to construct a rustic building for nature study. His budget was small, and he wanted to involve the Scouts in the actual construction, so the boys would feel it was truly their building. I suggested post-and-sill construction, which I illustrated with a few rough sketches. My friend adjusted his plan for small logs that the kids could cut and handle. They did less hewing, too, leaving more round log showing than is typical of post-and-sill construction, where all log faces are dressed off. Although it took longer to build with boy-power and boy-size logs, the result was more than satisfactory.

The post-and-sill technique is convenient these days because much pulpwood is shipped in hundred-inch lengths. A logger can set aside suitable logs of the species you desire and have them delivered to your building site. Post-and-sill walls use relatively short timbers, and long timbers are needed only for ceiling ties and rafters. A presentable version of post-and-sill construction is made even easier by purchasing eight-by-eight or ten-by-ten rough-sawn timbers and then hewing them with an adze and broadax on the exposed surfaces.

Virtually all original post-and-sill construction has been lost to fire, decay, age, and demolition. Some still exists under buildings that look conventional, because log or timbered houses were sometimes covered in clapboard or other siding. Indeed, you can develop an eye for quite plain old buildings that hide historic treasure inside.

Illustration of Orawski.

CHAPTER TWENTY

ORAWSKI

Another European influence on American log construction was the northern Slavic and Scandinavian tradition. For his best work, Croixsyde, Aldrich hired a team of Finnish log craftsmen whose log building reflected northern techniques. I have been told that Aldrich's Finnish crew was kept on the job at Croixsyde for almost three years, although Aldrich doesn't mention the length of time.

A regional source may be observed in the buildings at the Orawski Ethnographic Park in Poland, which I have visited. Orawski is in the foothills of the Tatra Mountains, a moderately rugged territory with an ample supply of logs. At least one of the log buildings in the park was constructed in the sixteenth century. The more recent traditional log houses were in use until they were moved to the park for preservation. In America we have very few old log structures still standing, but the large collection in Poland indicates that a tradition of sound building allows log buildings to survive for centuries.

Some buildings show steep roofs that lack chimneys. Smoke from cooking fires was simply vented up into the attic loft. From there it made its way out of the gable ends. A large smoky attic was an ideal place for storing foodstuffs, an environment that retarded spoilage and discouraged vermin. Indeed, the upper parts of these building were slowly smoke cured, in a process that probably contributed to their longevity. To an American, a tradition of getting without chimneys may seem primitive and inefficient, as our imaginations picture massive stone or brick fireplaces from the Colonial period. Many American pioneer shacks had chimneys of sticks and mud, but our romantic mindset insists on conjuring up images of huge fireplaces with towering chimneys.

Instead of piling rock or brick for fireplaces, the Poles built foundations.

Each of the Orawski buildings rests upon a stone platform that rises at least a foot from the ground. Those builders had to haul a lot of rock to create those elevated platforms. They understood that raised foundations play a foremost role in preserving log structures.

As another special feature, the typical Orawski building has galleries and storerooms in the attic, which overhung the main structure, giving additional protection to the support logs. With the base of the building securely insulated from the elements and the upper portions protected by thatch and smoke, the entire structure could last a long time. The Poles also fought decay with a wooden skirt on the building's base to deflect water. The protective skirt was much easier to replace than the underlying logs. The skirt was usually made of split light-grained wood, the way we make split shakes. Long shakes of thirty or more inches could protect most of the base of a building in only a few courses. In the bottom row the shakes were pointed so water would drip clear and not soak into the end grain, and I noticed a few roofs covered with pointed shakes.

Such construction requires a cooperative labor force and relatively settled conditions, so that people could invest large amounts of labor in these permanent domiciles, or dom in Polish. Interdependent village life was capable of making that sustained effort and of providing the necessary skills, experience, and work force. The ceiling in the typical Orawski dom is six or seven logs high, requiring substantial manpower to wrestle large logs for placement and fitting. In contrast, American pioneer shacks, dugouts, cabins, and lean-tos were constructed with limited manpower and without a cooperative village social structure. Most of the dom in Orawski are classified as peasant huts, but *they show a high degree of sophistication. These differences suggest much about the forces that shaped European and American attitudes.*

The buildings at Orawski are very attractive with their lofts, overhangs, steep stairs, massive logs, and thatched roofs. The interiors are simple and utilitarian, although one room was customarily reserved for special occasions and was whitewashed. You can derive ideas and designs for your own log cabin from these and other ethnic European styles developed by centuries of experience.

CHAPTER TWENTY-ONE

THE SNAIL

Some log-cabin dreams are much more demanding than others. The dream that led to the Snail cabin began with the arduous task of reaching the cabin's prospective site on remote Best Island, north of Armstrong, Ontario. The designer and builder of the Snail, Wendel K. Beckwith, was a successful inventor, and his log cabin was individualized to suit his own conceptions, whereas most of the log cabins described in this text were based upon more popular models. It is a long journey from the traditional and practical Orawski log dwellings to Beckwith's idiosyncratic innovations. But there are many eccentric individuals who fabricate idiosyncratic worlds of their own. A photograph in the National Geographic shows Beckwith as the successful "hermit," happily in harmony with his handcrafted home, where his meticulous design meant efficient living, at least for him.

The Snail was intended as a one-man abode that could be easily heated in the coldest weather. The design reflects Beckwith's philosophical musings and his hope of one day meeting the alien beings he believed visited his area regularly. To his way of thinking, the Snail was a perfect home, as circular and self-contained as a flying saucer. The Snail was Beckwith's survival vehicle, only it didn't move: the aliens were supposed to come to it.

As part of Beckwith's air-lock system, his outside door opened onto a short hall with a low wall running on the spiral line of the Snail. A few feet inside, at the end of the low wall, was the lower half of a door, intended to stop cold air from rushing in whenever he entered or left the Snail. Cold air, which is heavier than warm air, would travel along the hall floor and stop at the half door, like a flood stopped by a dam.

Beckwith began his construction layout with an ordinary fifty-five-gallon oil drum as a guide. Old fuel drums are common artifacts in many remote parts of the north where individuals stored fuel for the months when travel was out of the question. Beckwith must have been pleased with himself for having found a use for one of those ever-present reminders of civilization.

Like many another hermit, Beckwith decided to build the Snail partly underground. He claimed that he heated the Snail in the dead of winter with a single little spruce tree per day. Reliable witnesses have reported that the Snail was cozily comfortable during subzero weather, although Beckwith preferred rather cool indoor temperatures. Nevertheless, despite the practicality of life in the ground, logs decay in the moist earth, even with superb drainage. And repairs to the outside walls are hardly possible without tearing the whole building apart. Beckwith, awaiting the flying saucers to carry him to his real home, was not concerned with permanence.

Beckwith's design is impressive for its complexity and attention to detail. His little sheet-metal cone-shaped stove was a marvel of efficiency. The sheet metal was easily transported to the remote site, where Beckwith constructed the stove with simple hand tools. He placed it in a depression in the cabin floor so that the surrounding earth served as a heat sink that stored warmth. Many other features are as integrated as the heating system. His storage pits, special drawers, shelves, and items with multiple uses make the most of the limited space.

The wood-block floor is another innovation. Who would expect to find a parquet floor in an underground log cabin? For all the work that went into it, however, the floor was less than a complete victory. If you walked across it in stocking or bare feet, you had to wipe sand off your feet before putting on boots. Indeed, the whole cabin was gritty inside because of the floor. Grains of sand were constantly kicked loose, and they got into everything. Then, too, mice burrowed under the floor blocks, buckling them at random. One of the caretakers, who lived there after Beckwith's death, told me that he and his companion spent the better part of a day trying to fill the mouse holes with fresh sand and to re-level the floor, but they were never able to evict the mice, who continued to excavate at will.

The Snail worked very well for Beckwith, who was in tune with his creation and its purpose in his life. Those who follow are not apt to have the builder's harmony with the building. And so the Snail is an orphan without Beckwith to care for it. Fascinating as are the glimpses into Beckwith's life, the task of conserving or living with such remnants presents a challenge that most of us could do without. But the dreams of others can be inspiring, as your dreams lead you to conceive your own form of log cabin.

Plans of the Snail

General view of snail log building. Recessed into hill side and drawing warmth from the ground it uses about one fourth of the fuel wood for heating that a conventional log building built on the same site would consume. The woods surrounding the building are preserved as protection from the wind and to provide a deeply snow blanket for ground insulation in the natural manner. The roof is sodded with the natural carpet of moss and plants to insulate the roof snow from internal melting and heat loss. Brush surrounding the roof pockets snow upon it. The stone retainer walls facing the sun generate heat for added warmth.

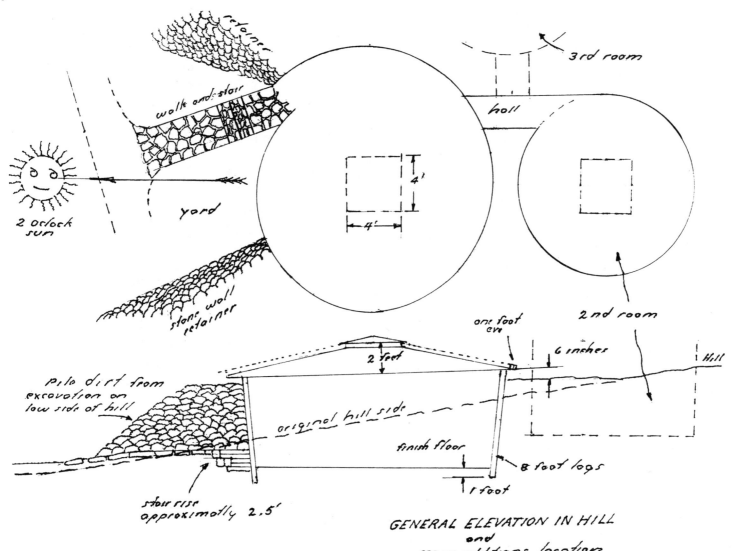

retainer

walk and stair

yard

2 o'clock sun

stone wall retainer

3rd room

hall

4'

4'

2nd room

one foot eve

6 inches

hill

2 feet

pile dirt from excavation on low side of hill

original hill side

finish floor

8 foot logs

1 foot

stair rise approximately 2.5'

GENERAL ELEVATION IN HILL
and
room additions location

LAYING OUT EXCAVATION

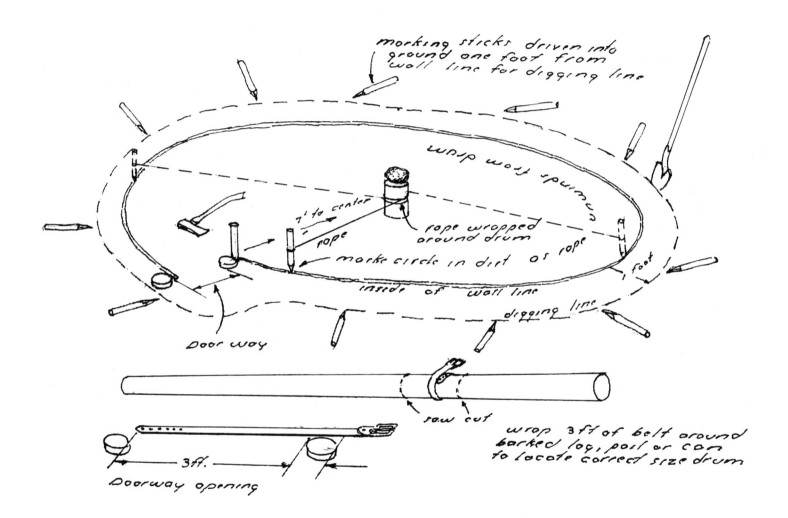

marking sticks driven into ground one foot from wall line for digging line

wrap rope from drum

7' to center

rope wrapped around drum

rope

marke circle in dirt os rope

foot

inside of wall line

digging line

Door way

saw cut

Doorway opening

3 ft.

wrap 3 ft of belt around barked log, pail or can to locate corred size drum

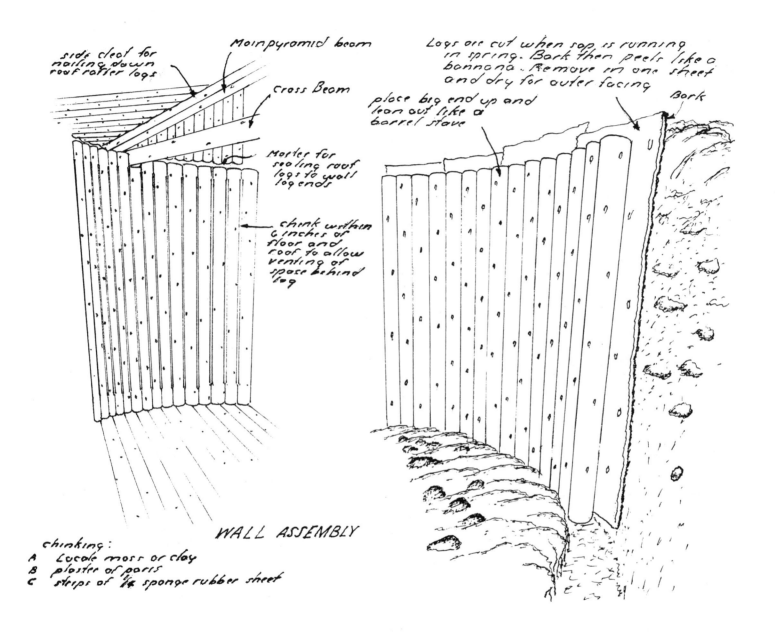

side cleat for
nailing down
roof rafter logs

Mainpyramid beam

Cross Beam

Morter for
sealing roof
logs to wall
log ends

chink within
6 inches of
floor and
roof to allow
venting of
space behind
log

Logs are cut when sap is running
in spring. Bark then peels like a
banana. Remove in one sheet
and dry for outer facing

place big end up and
lean out like a
barrel stave

Bark

WALL ASSEMBLY

chinking:
A   Locale moss or clay
B   plaster of paris
C   strips of ⅛ sponge rubber sheet

General view of snail ready for roofing over

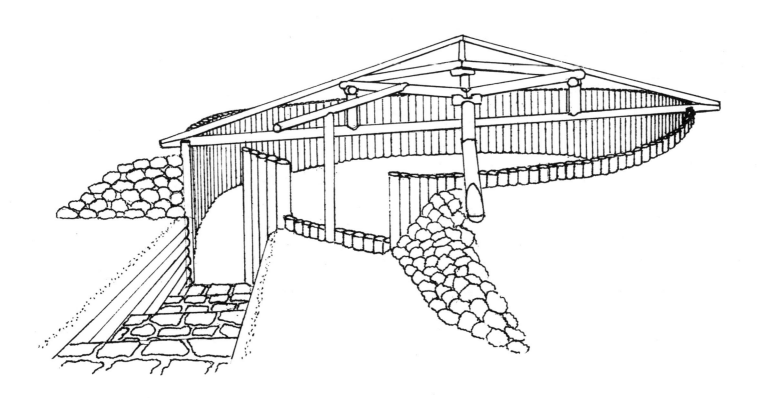

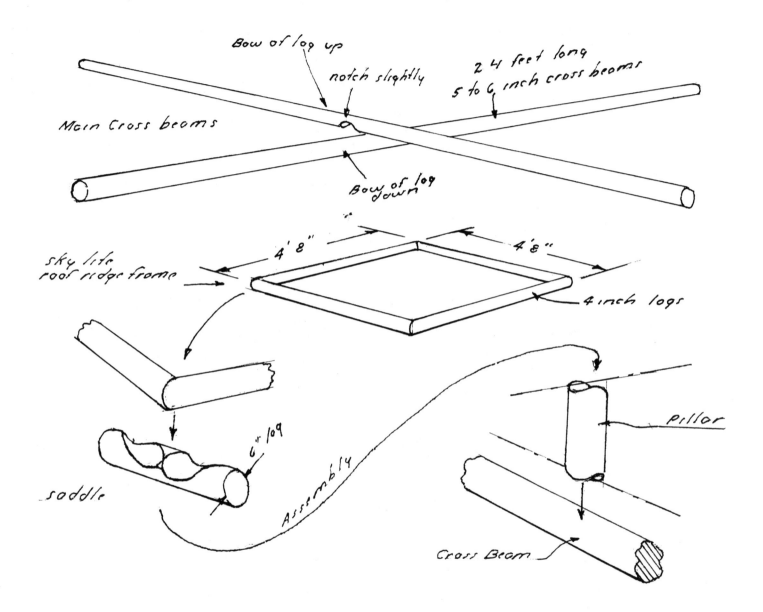

ROOF SUPER STRUCTURE

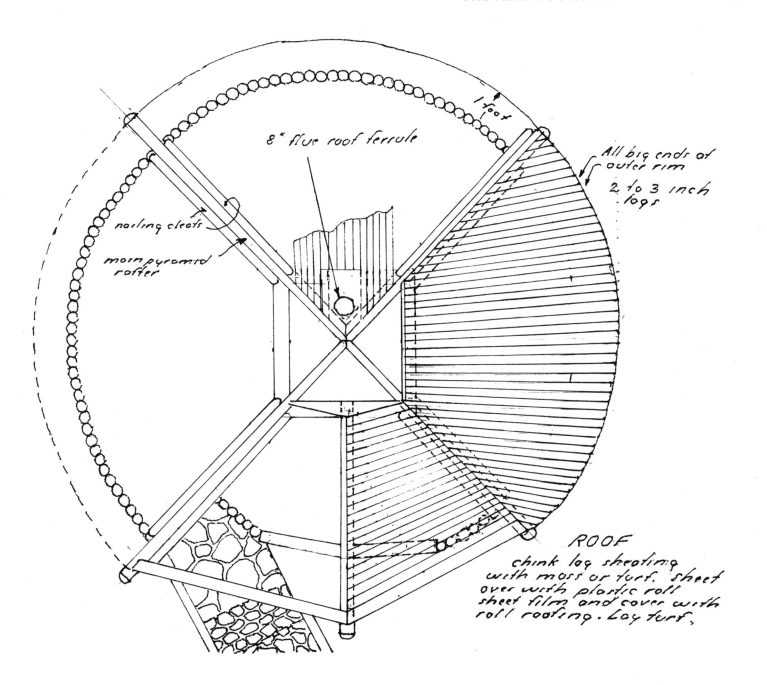

1 foot

8" flue roof ferrule

All big ends at
outer rim

2 to 3 inch
logs

nailing cleats

main pyramid
rafter

ROOF
chink log sheating
with moss or turf, sheet
over with plastic roll
sheet film and cover with
roll roofing. Lay turf,

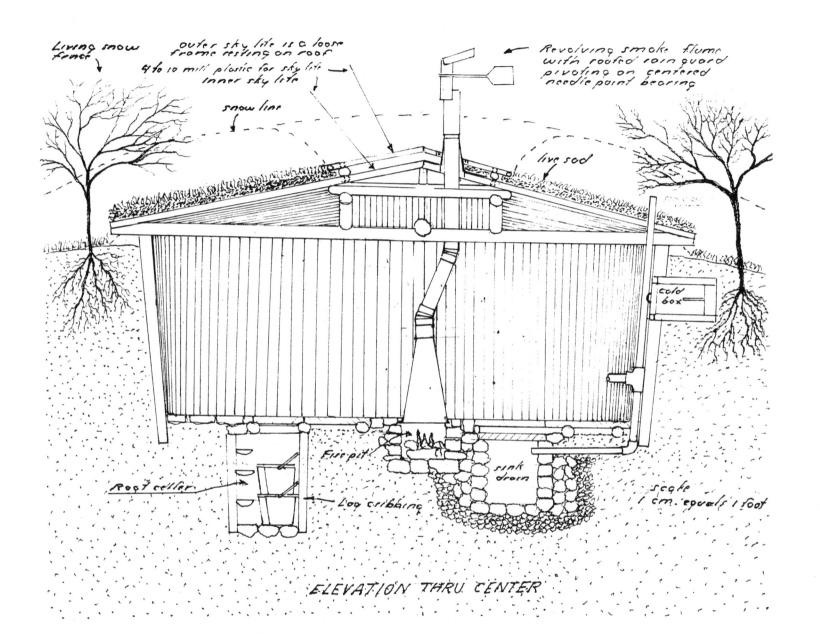

Living snow fence

outer sky lite is a loose frame resting on roof

4 to 10 mill plastic for sky lite

inner sky lite

snow line

Revolving smoke flume with roofed rain guard pivoting on centered needle point bearing

live sod

cold box

Fire pit

Root cellar

Log cribbing

sink drain

scale 1 cm. equals 1 foot

ELEVATION THRU CENTER

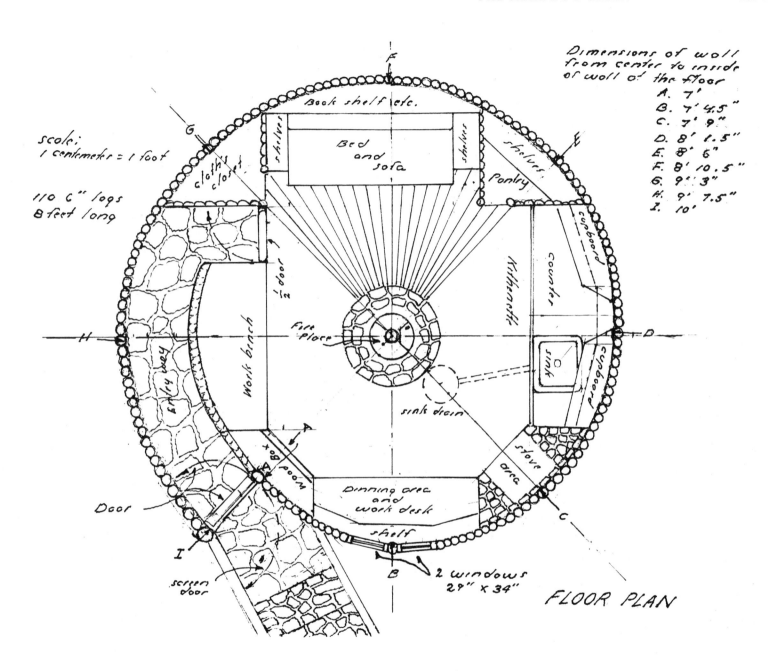

Dimensions of wall
from center to inside
of wall of the floor
A. 7'
B. 7' 4.5"
C. 7' 9"
D. 8' 1.5"
E. 8' 6"
F. 8' 10.5"
G. 9' 3"
H. 9' 7.5"
I. 10'

scale:
1 centimeter = 1 foot

110 6" logs
8 feet long

Book shelf etc.

shelves

shelves

shelves

Bed
and
sofa

clothes closet

Pantry

cupboard

counter

Kitchenette

door 1

door 2

Fire Place

Work bench

dry kitchen

sink drain

sink

cupboard

stove area

Door

Box wood

Dinning area
and
work desk

shelf

I

screen door

B

2 windows
29" x 34"

FLOOR PLAN

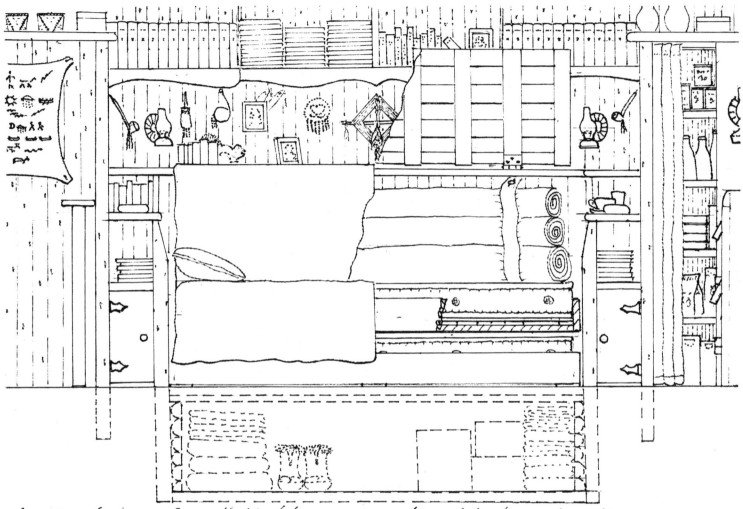

A - Day bed or sofa with blanket covering over hinged back and mattress
B - Hinged cushioned back in 'up' or bed time position
C - Upper mattress in frame serving as sofa and single bed (30").
D - Lower mattress in pull out frame to join upper mattress as double bed.
E - log chest for storage under sofa bed.
F - Roll bedding in current use stored behind sofa back.

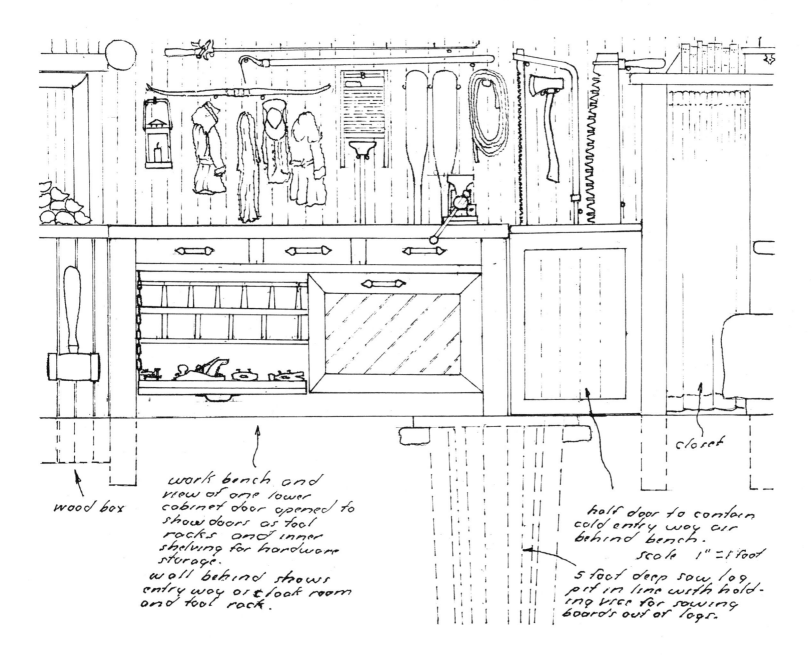

wood box

work bench and
view of one lower
cabinet door opened to
show doors as tool
racks and inner
shelving for hardware
storage.
wall behind shows
entry way or cloak room
and tool rack.

closet

half door to contain
cold entry way air
behind bench.
scale 1" = 1 foot
5 foot deep saw log
pit in line with hold-
ing tree for sawing
boards out of logs.

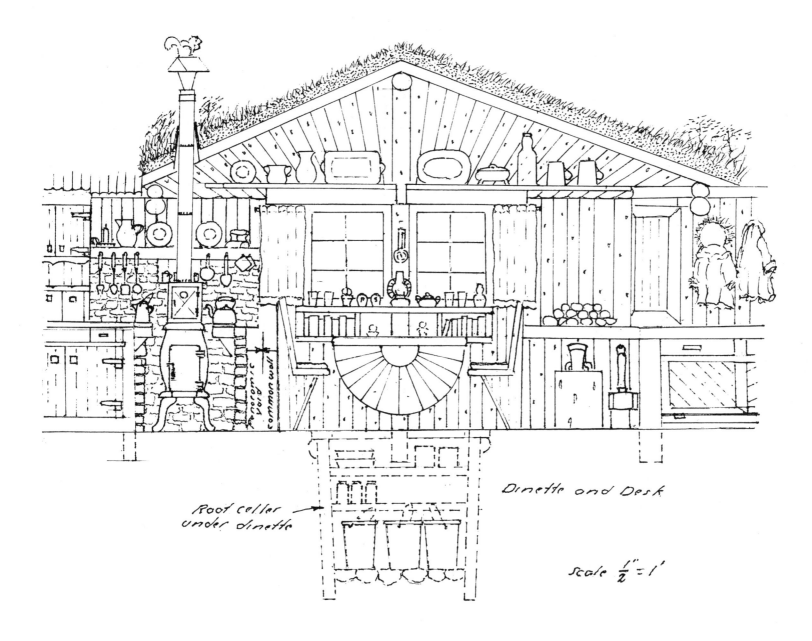

Pneumatic void

common wall

Root cellar
under dinette

Dinette and Desk

Scale $\frac{1"}{2} = 1'$

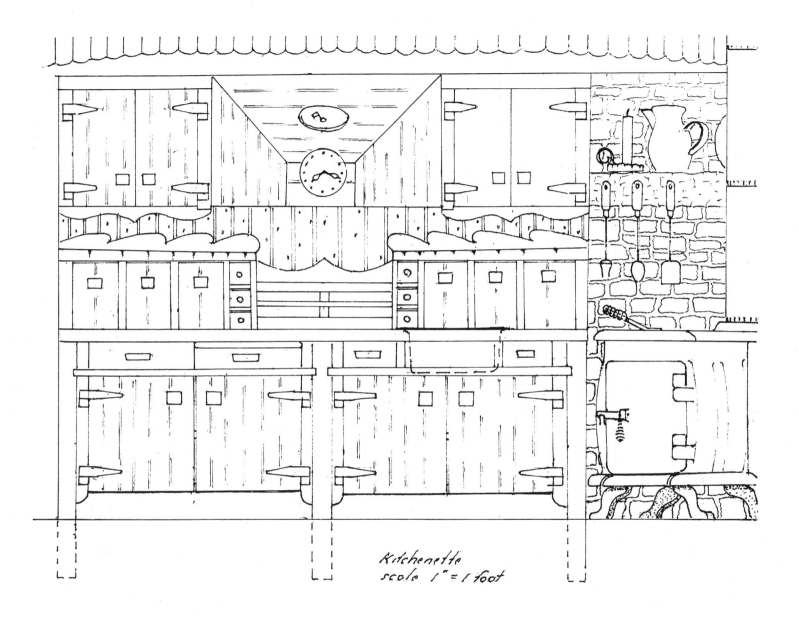

Kitchenette
scale 1" = 1 foot